The Love Letter That Changed EVERYTHING

Allisun Wilbur

First Paperback edition March 2021

Manufactured in the United States of America

Published by Victory Vision Publishing and Consulting, LLC
www.victoryvision.org

ISBN - 9798718470888

DEDICATION

This book is dedicated to my brilliant son, Kadin, whom I treasure. Thanks for pushing me to finish, by turning writing into a competition. I love you from God's beginning to never ending!

To my family whom I love deeply, I am eternally grateful for your prayers, support and love through the highs and the lows.

To all the individuals who selflessly shared their testimony or contributed in some way, I am so appreciative of you. The power you each carry, because of the transformative nature of Jesus, is beautiful and inspiring.

DEDICATION

CONTENTS

FOREWORD

Most of our lives have some sort of heartache or disappointment. The people in this book echo some of those challenging life moments. Reflecting the authentic journey's that these individuals have taken to bring them back to a place of hope, healing, or restoration. This book is a journey into the different lives of ordinary people who have made the extraordinary recovery to a normal, faith-filled life.

I believe you will enjoy this book as it is a short, easy read. I believe you will find the book may end up reading you in many ways. As I read, I found many parts I personally could relate to, maybe one per testimony. Those in the book found a combination of "grit" and faith that did more than carry them through. Sit back, read, and enjoy. See lives change.

I have known Allisun Wilbur for several years, she has always been able to look through circumstances and overcome them with a smile and a laugh that will change atmospheres. The hope she brings is contagious and I have found she lives life "all in".

~Bill Johnson
Founder of ProphetU
School of the Advancement of Prophetic People
ProphetU.com

INTRODUCTION

Love; a concept so hardwired into our DNA that it is as necessary as eating, drinking, or exercising. Scientifically, it has been linked to our health and life expectancy in many powerful ways. Like oxygen, it is non-negotiable. Wars have been fought over it, lives have been transformed by it, religions are substantiated by it, and quality of life is rooted within it. Whether defined as a choice, action, or emotion, love is often so complex that it can present itself as internally tangible.

The Greek language has at least four different words to describe love in a variety of different contexts; *agápe, éros, philía,* and *storgē. Agápe* is defined as unconditional love, *éros* is self-serving or sexual love, *philía* is brotherly love as it relates to friendship, and *storgē* is affection and love as between parents and children[1].

While other languages have multiple ways of defining and expressing love's different adaptations, we have only one word in English—one word to express the magnitude and complexity that love contains. So that one word must hold all the mystery and power of thriving, versus merely surviving. The question is posed, "What is the definition of love, and why is it important?" Here are some of the most popular responses from some in my closest circle, as well as some passersby. The importance of love is indisputable, and here is a glimpse into the why.

---

[1] (A 2020)

*"To be loved means to be unconditionally cared for. It is so important because we were made to love and be loved. I believe we would perish without it. We would not be able to thrive in any aspect." ~*Denise

*"It allows me to 'love' even when I don't 'like.' It fills me in a way nothing else does or can. It is essential because it allows me to have the mind of Christ towards people. It changes how I think and behave. If I am loving, I am happy. Love is what flows through me from the Holy Spirit that allows me to see someone as God sees them. It's the Creator's love for his children." ~*Lezlie

*"To me, love is a choice. It is not just an emotion. Yes, love can be moved by emotion but is it is a choice every day to serve someone, forgive someone, and be committed to the covenant of marriage or the commitment of friendship or the example of love to others as Christ flows freely out of us. Christ says love is the greatest commandment. Therefore, it is the most important thing we will ever do. He is our ultimate example of laying down His life and being unconditional with us." ~*Kasey

*"Love has a lot of different meanings to me. It is a feeling I get when I help a friend. It is watching a sunrise or sunset. It is understanding someone and having no way to explain it. It is giving someone your heart without expecting anything in return. It is hoping for theirs. Love is something to work for, get desperate for, and fight for. It should be brand-new every time it is felt. I am surrounded by it, but sometimes, it feels out of reach. Love is a connection—natural, and learned. I do not think you can see beauty without love. 1 Corinthians 13!" ~*Ty

"Love means waking up and choosing to love others. Love, to me, means compassion, heartfelt talks, loving when you had rather not. It also can mean being honest, guidance, security, acceptance, no matter what happens. Love also means forgiveness, sharing, not letting others go without when you know they are in need—forgiving, even when not forgiven, and investing in yourself. Love is important to me because I get to choose, and the time's I have chosen to love, I have seen changes in circumstances. I love feeling valued and accepted. I love to love others. Love is important because this is the antidote for all enemy schemes." ~Jennifer

"I think that love is someone who's going to stand by you and support you no matter what. Love is not giving up. Love is looking at someone you do not like at that moment and saying, 'I'd still do anything for you.' Love is intimacy. Love is laying down your own selfish needs and sacrificing what you need for the one you love. Love is God. Love is being honest. Love is saying the hard things. Love is accountability." ~Danielle

"Love is action; love is deciding to see the best and do the best for another person. Love is about not losing their heart to win an argument. It is about being selfless. Love makes you feel safe, secure, and 100% your true self. Love is to know and be known by another." ~Shellie

"When I think of love, I think of choice. I believe many people mistake love for an emotion, but some of the most important words that go behind 'love' for me would be kindness, cherish, trust, protect, God, pray for. It is important because it is in our DNA, and to deny love is like rejecting ourselves. When we withhold our love, we become bitter. It destroys us to withhold. When we lose love, it hurts

us, but when we give and receive it, we are carefree."
~Heather

"Unconditional affection, because without it, we will never feel worthy." ~Julie

The one word for love produces individualized parameters and expectations, defining its personalized meaning. These can be created from life experiences, both good and bad, examples set, our language for love, and even information learned. The difference between "I love chocolate" as opposed to "I love my family" or "I love my significant other" contrasts with "I love God." With the wide range of adaptations for the one powerful word, the thing that distinguishes all these connotations is its sustainable ability. There is a bold distinction between love and its inexact counterfeit infatuation. The most authentic, most powerful love will be gauged by its ability not to diminish or disappear. It is going to be 100% trustworthy, life-giving, consistent, and transformational.

We live in a society that is continually telling us, especially women, that to be successful, we must be strong and independent. This is not a bad thing on the surface but it can push people into a place of isolation where they are fighting to be worthy of unrealistic expectations that they set for themselves. If we get hurt, we shut down, putting up barricades and walls around our heart, making inner vows to ourselves that no one will be able to touch us again. Consequently, we live our lives on a surface level, being incredibly careful that nothing of substance penetrates our carefully crafted fortification.

Likewise, it has been ingrained in the male psyche by our culture that men must be tough, never show emotion, and never cry. Coincidentally, many (maybe even you) walk around feeling empty, depressed, and lonely. Desperation rises, almost subconsciously, from the desire to be seen but not having the courage to push past the fear of rejection. I would like to point out that it is no accident that God gave men tear ducts.

Suicide rates have skyrocketed because of this epidemic of what I call "love malnutrition." The definition of malnutrition is the condition that develops when the body does not get the right amount of vitamins, minerals, and other nutrients it needs to maintain healthy tissues and organ function. Similarly, when our body does not gain or give the right amount of love, it becomes malnourished and does not function how it was designed. This can affect not only the body, but the mind, emotions, and spirit, thus putting the afflicted in a place of mental separation and helplessness.

An article written by The FP Group, entitled *America's Suicide Epidemic Is a National Security Crisis*[2] explains, "The National Center for Health Statistics recently released a major study, examining the national trends in suicide. The results are grim: The age-adjusted suicide rate in the United States increased a staggering 24 percent from 1999 to 2014. Increases were seen in every age group except for those 75 and above and in almost every racial and gender category. The national rate rose to 13 deaths per 100,000 people in 2014. Contrast that now with homicide, which killed 5.1 Americans per 100,000 in 2013.[3] We instinctively fear the murderer

---

[2] (Deboer 2016)

[3] (Centers for Disease Control and Prevention n.d.)

hiding in the bushes, but we are at far greater risk from ourselves."

While it may be hard to nail down a specific all-encompassing definition of love, love's health benefits are easy to identify, much more apparent, and can be tangibly experienced. Love produces positive emotions; one of the most wonderful is laughter.

As stated by the Huffington Post[4] "It [laughter] is a very powerful antidote to fight stress, conflict, and pain both mentally and physically. Love also has the power to heal and renew one's mental, emotional, and physical well-being. Research shows that loving acts neutralize the kind of negative emotions that adversely affect immune, endocrine, and cardiovascular function." Love can even help to keep the doctor away and fight diseases. Studies have proven that patients diagnosed with cancer react to and recover from cancer treatment faster when they have strong family connections. According to the *National Institute of Health[5]*, love triggers the hormone *oxytocin*, making us feel good. It also lowers the levels of stress chemicals in our system.

So, if love is the answer that makes us superhuman both mentally and physically, why are so many people missing it? I believe the most straightforward answer is that as humans, we are flawed, imperfect, self-serving, and self-critical. Therefore, when it comes to loving others and even loving ourselves, we fail time after time. Our society has booming businesses catering to people trying to make themselves good enough. People are literally dying to feel acknowledged and loved. Maybe it is not a facelift, but a

____

4 (Thaik 2013)
5 (Carter and Porges 2012)

spiritual lift that we need. Perhaps missing years of our life could be traded for moments of meaningful purpose as we become the absolute best at our job. Conceivably, instead of trying to cover up our unique features with hundreds of dollars of makeup products or steroids to pump through our veins, we need to be seen and recognized just as we are.

Nevertheless, there is good news! The good news on which this book's foundation rests firmly upon; there is a better source of love. One that does not come from imperfect individuals, possessions, or accomplishments. This love is pure love, unconditional love, forgiving love, a selfless love, a love not based on performance or perfection. This love can change everything!

This love has a name; it is God. Love is not merely an attribute of God, but it *is* His fundamental nature. In the Bible, 1 John 4:8 says, *"Whoever does not love does not know God, because God is love."* (NIV)

There are many facets to the love of God, according to 1 Corinthians 13: *"If I speak with human eloquence and angelic ecstasy but don't love, I'm nothing but the creaking of a rusty gate. If I speak God's Word with power, revealing all his mysteries and making everything plain as day, and if I have faith that says to a mountain, 'Jump,' and it jumps, but if I don't love, I'm nothing. If I give everything I own to the poor and even go to the stake to be burned as a martyr, but I do not love, I have gotten nowhere. So, no matter what I say, what I believe, and what I do, I am bankrupt without love. Love never gives up. Love cares more for others than for self. Love does not want what it does not have. Love doesn't strut, doesn't have a swelled head, doesn't force itself on others, isn't always 'me first', doesn't fly off the handle, doesn't keep*

We are all created with a piece missing that God fits perfectly into. He designed us to choose Him because authentic love always starts with a choice. Until we discover His authenticity, we feel off, like something is missing. From my own experiences and the testimonies of the multiple people I interviewed on my writing journey, the same theme weaved throughout. We know God as real, not because of religion or somebody telling us what to believe, nor out of habit or fear. We came to a crossroads of experiencing the Creator of the universe for ourselves. We realized His desire to know us and be heard by us. Being filled with the truest of love creates the most tangible, irreversible, and powerful experiences of our life. He came in and exposed what had been hidden, healed what was broken, brought joy to the depressed, removed the self-hate that had been lingering, and showed Himself as All-Knowing, All-Powerful, and All-Loving. Everyone's experience of how the reality of God came alive in their life is different, but one thing is for certain; the legitimacy is irrefutable in their spirit.

God's unique facets are limitless and most definitely would not fit between this book's covers, no matter how large we make it. This book will explore a few of these facets or personality traits that I have gotten to know of God. This has come through my personal relationship with His Son, Jesus Christ, and made tangible by the power of the Holy Spirit. It is those unique traits that allow everyone to be able to have compelling and unique experiences with Him. He can reach an individual when they need Him most and be able to meet their need. The power of God negates coincidence and enforces confirmation. There are many times in my life when I needed God, the Great Physician. Other times I needed the God Who could see me when I felt forgotten. Still others I needed God, the Victor. This book has many interviews with people who truly experienced God in vastly different, yet equally powerful, ways. The only common denominator to having a genuine experience with God is a willing and open heart.

You do not have to have it all figured out. You can still be full of questions, doubts, and negative strongholds about this "Christian nonsense." Or, by contrast, you might be head over heels in love with Jesus and be passionately pursuing Him. Maybe you're somewhere in the middle. Wherever you are today, as you hold this book in your hand, you have value. I pray you keep reading with an open mind, open heart, and open spirit. Perhaps this is the love letter, written just for you, that will change everything.

CHAPTER ONE
LOVING THE FORGOTTEN

Letters have had a foundational and boundless importance throughout history. Fascination with these vital means of communication, before the technological era took over, has remained steadfast. Covering a vast collection of information pertaining to corporate business, family connections, intimate affairs, religious discoveries, and public matters, by no surprise, the love letter has remained the apex of letter writing. Far beyond the wording, these precious letters symbolize so much more, such as time and attention, affection printed in words that are not regularly expressed, and the effort of the loved one eagerly detailing the matters of the heart. The beautiful stories of transcriptions from brave soldiers traveling to their eager lovers and then back again can make you weak in the knees. I was pondering this passionate display of love; profound, abiding, intentional, lifesaving. Is there any greater love?

Yes! The mystical force of God's perfect love far supersedes our imagery or our humanistic grasp of love. He is infinite, eternal, and never changing. As He created the universe and us along with it, He did so with a specific strategy in mind. You see, God is Love, and His love is the reason He created us. He breathed us into existence because of love, with the primary purpose being to be loved. That is absolutely mind-blowing if you dare to believe it! We were created to be loved by our Heavenly Father and to be an expression of that love to others.

Throughout this book, you will hear different pieces of my story and testimony. Still, I want to start with what I call *the* moment—the moment that religion shifted into a relationship, and I heard my Heavenly Father speak to me through words I did not recognize in a notebook in front of me. These words stared back at me, and as I read and reread them, tears streamed down my face, and laughter burst forth because, at that moment, they were way more than just words. In an instant, I realized that not only was God real, but He loved me despite my many flaws and imperfections. He desired a relationship with me in the face of my unfaithfulness. He was okay with me being real and was willing to answer my tough questions. At that moment, I needed God to see me and respond.

I did not need blind Christian faith, tied with the religious bow. Stamp-your-ticket-Sunday-put-a-bumper-sticker-on-your-car-and-maybe-wear-a-Jesus-ball-cap was no longer enough. I was at the point of putting it all on the line, and through my tears, I was literally screaming at Heaven, demanding God show Himself! I was at the place of "all-in" or "all-out" because I simply was not designed to ride the fence of hypocrisy. I could not "fake it till I made it" because I was losing and was lost in every capacity. This is not how I envisioned my life going. I had been at this crossroad before, several years earlier, and the wrong choice had taken me far from God. Pain, shame, anger, and a lack of identity accompanied me on a path of self-destruction while I tried to fix my life all on my own. I forgot who I was as I drove myself deeper into a place where I was very confident even God had forgotten about me.

(I am here to tell you that it was a lie from the pit of hell! God is capable of meeting us in our ugly without

condemnation or judgment. God's heart is for the forgotten. His love is that big!)

As I cried out to God, asking Him to show Himself as real and tangible, I had no idea what to expect. I half anticipated to be struck down by lightning as the fire and brimstone God stood over me, bellowing, "Is that real enough?" The other half of me confident that He wouldn't even come through. Nevertheless, deep in my spirit, I knew that others had experienced amazing encounters with this Father God, so I held onto my "mustard seed of faith" and kept praying and asking.

Then, after what felt like an eternity, God came through just for me because His heart is for me and not against me. The lights didn't flicker; the wind didn't rush through the house, and an angel didn't descend and declare, "Thus says the Lord!" All those things might as well have happened because the touch and voice of God were so real in my spirit. I'll never forget that moment.

I picked up the pen sitting next to me and wrote with an intensity and persistence that shocked me. It was not until I finished writing when I went back and reread the words that had just hit the paper. I was a hot mess, but the joy of the Lord hit me so hard, I could not stop laughing as I read the words out loud, tears pouring down my face. For the first time in my life, I heard God speak. I felt true value. I knew He did not forget about me and that He loved me no matter what!

Below is the love letter that God wrote to me that day, but it has taken on a new form since then. As I mentioned before, God created us to be loved by Him, but then we are to take that expression of love and bestow it to others. We become transformed into a physical love letter to all His sons and daughters, which includes you. *(Yes, you too!)* May the words come alive in your heart and spirit as you hear His loving voice speak directly to you.

My Child,

Be still and know that I am God. Be still and know that I am your God, and I can speak directly to you. Be still and let Me minister to you, not as a religion, but as your Heavenly Father. I speak to you today to let you know you are loved, you are precious, you are beautiful, and you are good enough. You have not been forgotten.

I see your hurt and shame, I see your wounds and pain, and I am not ashamed of you. Lift your downcast eyes, and know your worth. You have been fought for, you have been sacrificed for, and you have been loved for longer than you realize. Embrace Me and feel My unconditional love pour over you, washing away every blemish and imperfection that the cruel world has attached to you.

You have so much anger and unforgiveness stored up over a lifetime of battling to survive. Lay down your weapons, break down the walls, and stand before Me, vulnerable and ready to let it all go. This is not easy, but it is worth it! Smother your anger with peace, so the fire which destroys will destroy no more. Forgive, so the unforgiveness will cease to poison you another moment.

It is not okay that you were hurt. It is not okay that My sweet child was wounded. It is not okay that you felt trapped, and the lies Satan whispered to you that were so convincing were not okay. But for every "not okay," I have the power to heal and restore. I sacrificed My perfect Son, Jesus Christ, so that you could have the chance to choose Me.

You may be angry at Me, shamelessly directing your disgust My way, asking for answers as to why I let this happen to you; that is okay. I am your Heavenly Father, and I can handle your anger. Please know and understand that I was not the cause! I was there and will continue to be right there with you through it all. Every question will not have an answer, but I feel your pain, and I cry for you, My child.

Your freewill makes you unique, and from the beginning of man's creation, I have never changed My mind that My design is good. Your choices are yours and yours alone, but no matter what wrong turns you make, what sins you commit in the darkness, you will never be passed over or forgotten. It is never too late; you can still return to Me. A single sin is no more terrible than any other sin, and we will simply recalibrate your life's compass. I will use even the worst of sins for My glory.

*Have faith in Me that while it seems hopeless, unfair, and you're suffocating, **I am here!** When you do not think that you can handle anything else, My strength is with you and **in** you. You do not have to tackle it all alone. Your test will write your testimony. Even those tests you feel you flunked. There is hope in the darkness as you search for my light. I am pleased with your searching.*

I call to you, My child, right now, just as you are, not as you feel you should be. Lay down the anger, confusion, depression, sadness, unforgiveness, and moments where your "why" is tested. Lay it down at the feet of your Heavenly Father, Creator of the Universe, for I will take care of it. As a

Father to the fatherless, I am here to fill the void, which causes so many questions and provides unmatchable security. You are My world. You do not fit in a box to be compared with others around you. You are free to be who I created you to be. Use your talents for My glory.

Look at your past with different eyes; for while it helps shape who you are, it does not define who you will be! The tears you cry are beautiful to Me, so do not feel ashamed to let them flow. I am the Potter, and you are the clay. Your tender tears are the water I use to soften my clay to make it moldable and useful. Your tears allow hurt and pain to flow from you into My hands, making it possible to form you into a strong and majestic masterpiece. Out of you, My light will shine for the world to see.

Take heart, for I am specifically and intimately personal, and I see the missing piece of your puzzle. The piece that died, was stolen, given away, hidden, or lost. I know the ache you feel as you realize how precious that puzzle piece was and is. I will fill that void with My love, grace, and mercy, and you will no longer feel as if you are lacking.

You cannot change the past but, through our relationship, you have been equipped with the power and authority of Jesus Christ to overcome that evil, which has been strangling the life out of you, with good. Take on each challenge with renewed courage and faith. Know I am there! Raise the bar you have set for yourself, run your race, and fulfill your destiny. Do not wait for your conditions to change; start today. Trust in the faith I have in you. Walk out the purpose I carefully designed you for. Know that I care; know there is nothing you have done or will do that will keep Me from loving you. I made you with every quirk and uniqueness. You are not simple or ordinary. You are My masterpiece, a jewel in the King's crown.

You are extraordinary, and I love you today, right now, right where you are!

Love for all of eternity,

> *Your Abba Father, your God, your King,*
> *your Creator, your Biggest Fan!*

As I read these words staring up at me, I realized it was not God who had forgotten me; rather, I had forgotten and lost sight of Him and needed to remember who I was. I have learned that God can take me to places within myself that hours of speculation or meditation could never reach. It's like having a personal guide while navigating the terrifying tundra of my psyche—a journey of discovery within myself as He orchestrates the direction of my next step. In every breath, every moment, every step, every word, every stroke of my pen, I need God. I need Him not because I am weak, but because I am strong enough now to invoke assistance. He is my game plan and final answer. My blueprint is revealed through a beautiful scavenger hunt of connections. He draws me into a relationship with Him, making me continuously dependent. He does not give me every answer, but like breadcrumbs, I follow the tangible, and yet unseen, on the most exciting journey of my life. The Creator of the Universe takes the ordinary and injects the extraordinary, allowing me to go places I never dreamed possible and experience the joy I never thought plausible. Words transcribed from pen to paper can be illiterate illusions, void of substance or fortitude. However, when Holy Spirit inflames and ignites the lifeless utterance, it instantly jumps off the page, vivaciously, coming to life in a beautiful harmony of truth and hope. The voice of God no longer seems so distant and abstract. The reality of His love is intentionality pressing in.

While the past may not look as I envisioned, the adventure is worth every plot twist. As I do life with passion, He maneuvers me and guides me to the absolute best of everything predestined for me. As I lose the words to describe the radiance of the Lord, He fills my white pages with life-giving ink. Words possessing resurrection power are no longer straightforward linguistics, but the "bread of life" and heartbeat of Heaven, flavored with the sweet breath of a very tangible God.

When I stop passionately pursuing my Heavenly Father and decide subconsciously that I am far enough, have done enough, or have it covered, my weary spirit ends up in the fight for my life with no allies. I go chasing a devil unaided and end up chased by the same monster. I may attempt to convince myself that I am big enough to take on my adversary solo, but I am not! Stepping fully out of self or religion and fully into relationship, takes the comfort out of our journey. It pushes the individual to a place that requires nothing but courage and engaged hope. We may sing the songs, raise our hands, and make enthusiastic declarations saying, "Yes, Lord!" Even with this, can you trust our Heavenly Father to step out of the fake and into authentic? Will you go past the onslaught of contention and judgment? Will you take the leap from comfort into the reality of your authentic design?

It is beautiful to me how God can see us, all of us, and still see the potential we possess. No matter what part of our journey we are on, or the weaknesses and flaws we see in ourselves, our Heavenly Father still chooses us. The Bible was given to us as a guide to life, but how do we relate to it when it is full of larger-than-life characters? Perhaps upon closer inspection, the individuals were flawed, imperfect human beings, saying yes to a larger-than-life God. Without applying the view of God's grace, and looking from the flawed perspective; Abraham was too old, Isaac was a daydreamer, Jacob was a liar, Leah was ugly, Joseph was abused, Gideon was afraid, Sampson was a womanizer, Rahab was a prostitute, Jeremiah and Timothy were too young, David had an affair and was a murderer, Elijah was suicidal, Isaiah preached naked, Jonah ran from God, Naomi was a widow, Job went bankrupt, Peter denied Christ, the disciples fell asleep while praying, Martha worried about everything, the Samaritan woman was divorced, Zacchaeus was too small, Paul was too religious, Timothy had an ulcer, and Lazarus was dead. Amongst all these imperfect people, God was able to save all of humanity, shift nations, ignite His church, raise up kings, prophets, and lovers of Christ and demonstrate His power through miracles, signs, and wonders.

Hear me correctly on this; I am not condoning sin. I wholeheartedly believe that as we come into the fullness of relationship with Christ, He loves the sin right out of us and causes us to desire change. No matter where you are at this very moment, you are in the perfect place to allow the All-Knowing into your life. God never calls the qualified, but He qualifies the called. You are called from the darkness to the light of more—the light of potential and the light of hope. You are not forgotten, but perhaps you have been saved for such a time as this.

I do not want to be what everyone wants me to be. I want to walk in the clarity of authenticity. I have the freedom to simply exist, but who knew what a challenge that could generate. God has met me in the place of numbness, understood me in the place of loss, and has soothed me in the place of discomfort. I have hope because my Father hands me optimism. I have anticipation because I know everything that He constructs is good, and I have reinvented joy for this new season of development.

I am learning that not everything removed is a loss, but a perspective shift when done by the loving hand of the Father. These shifts are not a punishment but rather a blessing escorting me to new certainties. As my mind spins from the reality of the overhaul that is taking place in my soul, I will cling to the Lord of Heaven and seek the promises that I have long thought too good to be true. I pray the bold prayers I have been too afraid to pray. I have permission to do so, but for God to answer them, I must lay out the blueprints of potential so that he can color in the hues of destiny. The breath of the Creator of the universe rushes over me, releasing me from the catatonic, statuesque state and freeing me from my own intentions. I step away from settling and strap in for preparation for my world to be rocked.

Therefore, I step into this season of vulnerable submission because I am not forgotten. I am more determined than ever to take risks, make messes, get it wrong, be embarrassed, and fall on my face because even so, I will do every bit of it authentically! I will not fake one moment of my idiosyncratic nature, finding my footing and leapfrogging from where I have been to where and who I am meant to be. I take this leap because I made a vow to be all-in. I pray as I get uncomfortable, it will permit others to find their authenticity and remember who they are and whose they are.

With this same spirit of vulnerability in mind, I transition slightly. I mentioned in the introduction that I interviewed many people on the journey to fashioning this book. In my mind, that was never the plan, but when you write a book about the authentic, tangible nature and love of God, He wants editor rights.

***

So, enter stage right, the first individual to share their heart and genuine experience with God.

"There was a time after I was separated and divorced from my ex-husband, that I would go to Palo Duro Canyon, and I would just tell the Lord, 'God, I need to be with you. Will you please meet me at the Canyon?' And He would because He is so good.

He would show up in different symbolic ways, whether it was a bunch of turkeys on the side of the road, or the clouds looking different that day. One time, He showed up as a deer alongside one of the cliffs. He was breathtaking and majestic.

It was not long after that I had a dream, and in the dream, I was on that same cliff with a man. We were laughing, and I was so happy. Suddenly, he said, "I love spending time with you!" and he kissed me on the forehead. Wow!

Time stopped because that was a joy I have not felt in a long time. It took me a while, but I finally figured out that it was Jesus. He does hear me, He does see me, and He does feel the pain.

Despite what may come my way, Jesus is there for me and He loves me more than anyone ever could."

~Anonymous

As seen in this testimony, when you have a true revelation of who God, Jesus, and Holy Spirit are and you see Their intentionality towards your life, it is revolutionary. It is not important whether you know anything about Him because His mind is still on you. In an instant, you can go from wanting to be unseen to being all in and hungry for more. The moment you see, feel, and know the Heavenly Father's heart for you, everything changes. Authentic love is truly illuminating and transformational.

CHAPTER TWO
IRONIC DUALITY

For through Him, we both have access to the
Father by one Spirit.

Ephesians 2:18 (NIV)

I keep asking that the God of our Lord Jesus
Christ, the glorious Father, may give you the
Spirit of wisdom and revelation, so that you
may know Him better. I pray that the eyes of
your heart may be enlightened in order that
you may know the hope to which He has called
you, the riches of His glorious inheritance in
His holy people.

Ephesians 1:17-18 (NIV)

"Today I have made you a fortified city, an iron
pillar and a bronze wall to stand against the
whole land - against the Kings of Judah, its
officials, its priests and the people of the land.
They will fight against you but will not
overcome you, for I am with you and will
rescue you," declares the Lord.

Jeremiah 1:18-19 (NIV)

Life is somewhat ironic, with its consistent and repetitive duality, extremes that often elevate us to a place of understanding, a new level of truth, while experiencing the opposite, to better understand its counterpart. To further complicate life, these dualities are not simply opposite but also complementary. They do not cancel each other out; they merely balance each other like the dual wings of a bird.

We are facing death, which gives us a better awareness of life—coming to know ugliness, just to be able to see beauty explode onto the page. It is always there, but dulled into submission by a life desperately being survived; a love internalized that can somehow uproot hatred, creating a triumphant crescendo of beauty. It is depression creeping in, like the water level rising and suffocating us until, with one last gasp, we remember we can swim and find the joy once forgotten.

The irony of these desperate lows and fantasized highs is you cannot have the positive without the negative. They are irreversibly woven together into a pattern of unveiled consistency. What would be perceived as the negative is effectively adding a new color to the spectrum of our sepia shaded lives. This vexation arises in the physical and emotional anguish we think we must go through to find the gemstones of understanding or the proverbial golden ticket!

So often, we stay transfixed, petrified in this place of hell, unable to turn the knob and walk through the door of epiphany. We remain glued in place, staring at the horror before us, consuming us. Those unknown possibilities are just out of reach, just beyond where we are, in dire need of a next step. We morph into a martyr of our past and present, which robs us of the future, and of the next chapter of promises yet discovered.

This is the place where we *must* become brave! Our hope must outweigh our hopeless spirit. In order to experience a new normal, our desire for more needs to outweigh our contrite disposition for a better future. If we stay in the pit of despair, all we will ever see is the misery of the four walls closing in. Instead, we could see the expanse of originality and beauty that is one step ahead. As we move, often painfully, onward, we create a momentum of something extraordinary that encourages others to follow in the wake. Are we willing to "pony up" or to "flex our brave" and open ourselves up to the absolute best version of ourselves?

We deserve it! We need to begin to despise all the lies we often believe and *stop* listening. We deserve to look at the horizon and believe that it can be formed into our wildest dreams. We deserve to watch the glass ceilings melt away, revealing possibilities, and boldly step into the realm of the unknown, advancing to something more, creating something new, opening lenses, and seeing with new perspectives. We deserve to be audacious.

It takes heart to pursue strength with everything you have. As you trudge through the quicksand valley of tribulation, you never start out with the strength. That is why Philippians 4:13 states, *"I can do all things through Christ who strengthens me."* Life sometimes does give us more than we can handle, but never more than God can handle. If you stare at these grains of misadventure and get frozen by the terrifying, yet never answered: "Why?" then look up and see the "collateral beauty" in *all* things, not just in good or easy and fair things, but see the goodness and redemption extended to you by your Heavenly Father.

***

Kelly had to come to a place of doing just that, seeing the beauty in his circumstances. Regardless of his choices,

God still had grace and love to pursue him no matter how far he ran. This testimony of reconciliation, amid life's duality, makes him a powerhouse of authority for the Kingdom because "he was lost, but now he is found."

"At 15 years of age, I had a God encounter. Up until that point, my knowledge and understanding of God had been casual. Random questions that my church-going grandma asked had piqued my interest but did not captivate my heart. My art teacher was the one who led me to the Lord Jesus at a teen outing. Leading me through the sinner's prayer, he helped shift me to a place of fully understanding the sacrifice Jesus made for me. He regularly picked me up for church on Sunday. It was after one of these Sundays when I was sitting in the living room by myself, flipping through the channels on the TV. I was hoping to find cartoons, but unfortunately, there weren't any on, so instead, I just zoned out to a church service that was on.

After watching for a few minutes, the camera zoomed in on the Bible to better view a verse that the pastor was preaching about. Now, my mind was drifting. I turned again to look at the TV, and suddenly, the words on the Bible formed into the face of Jesus. I was transfixed by this vision but, at the same time, afraid. The face was clearly seen and was made from the words in the Bible. From His eyes, nose, beard, like a well-shaped shadow, I could make out the face of Jesus. Upon looking at the face, everything in my heart said it was Jesus.

Untrained about spiritual things, it would be years before I completely understood that event. I would go through many heartfelt trials as a young man drifting away with no one to help. I would land in prison at a young age. It was there the vision would become the revelation.

I fell away from God and went to prison for the next eighteen years. In the cold dark cell, Jesus came to me again. He said, 'Look at you, back to where you started.' I began to cry and repented. My relationship with the Lord became more powerful than I had ever known before, and after restoration, the anointing was even more powerful. There were visual signs that even the other guys in prison noticed. My attitude, behavior, and the level of peace and joy shifted inside me. There were times when I could sense the Spirit so strong; it was like the presence of Jesus was my roommate because He was that tangible!

The way the glory of God was on me and the incredible prayer life He cultivated in me was honestly what got me through. There were so many miracles I got to see take place behind those walls, including a man who had heart disease get totally healed after I prayed for him. People sometimes say that they feel "drunk" in the Holy Spirit. I have never felt that sensation stronger than one day through a simple children's song in prison. I heard a song on the radio with the lyrics, 'Tell the world that Jesus loves you. Tell them you have found a forever friend. You have opened your heart's door to Him. The love of Jesus has no end.'[6] *With the heart of a child, I sang these lyrics over and over, continuing with my duties of the day. As I sang, I became intoxicated with the Holy Spirit. I could not even talk to anyone the whole day. It was such a beautiful moment, and I never wanted to get out of that place. Everything else just faded away as I soaked in the joy of the Lord.*

---

[6] (Card 1983)

I do not feel like I would have made it those eighteen years without Jesus. When I got out that time, I never went back or fell into those old habits again. This is not to say life was perfect, but I honestly believe that my pitfalls helped me stay connected to God. When we go through those valley moments, God is there, connecting with us and guiding us through. If life is all 'hunky-dory,' we will miss some of the greatest lessons and moments.

The greatest thing I have learned from life so far is that it is not about how good I am or how bad I am; it is all about God's love working through me in Christ Jesus. By walking with this mindset, in the fourteen years since I got out, there has never been a time where I have gone without feeling or experiencing God's presence. I do not regret prison. Hear me correctly that I regret what I did to get to prison, but I do not regret my time there. It was there I would begin an intimate relationship with Christ Jesus. God was able to take my pitfall and prison experience and turn it into my spiritual experience. I became the founder of a powerful prayer ministry, where people found powerful answers to prayers, saw visions, and could hear His voice. His gifts and callings on our lives never change, and He will meet you no matter what your circumstances are and allow you to flourish if you let Him. It all boils down to God's grace. It is not about what we know, what we give, how much we go to church or pray. It's all about God's grace through it all."

~Kelly

Life's uncomfortable and, at times, agonizing moments can almost become familiar and comfortable without the desire to change. Often, society is so eager to prescribe another pill, it encourages us to a place of complacency and dilutes our fight. We convince ourselves this is as good as it gets, and we forfeit our vision of the next level. Then suddenly, the moment hits, and you desire to reach out. The fog lifts as you reach for the impossible, pulling yourself out of the "normal" and to a place where nothing will ever look or feel the same again. When stepping out of a religious mindset and into the reality of God, one can no longer deny the presence of good and evil. At some point, any believer will come to an understanding and awareness of a spiritual battle that is taking place around us. This is present and very real whether we wish to acknowledge it or not.

***

Contrary to the world's perspective, ignorance is most definitely not bliss. Through his testimony, Matthew can explain the reality of experiencing the duality of life's lows and highs. His experience is nothing short of a spiritual awakening. He came face to face with the facts and was able to choose the truth and the love of his Heavenly Father, to set him free.

"It started one night when I was in my sophomore year of college, and I was already taking a hard class load. Baylor, my girlfriend, was pregnant at the time, and we were soon to get married. I was into Adderall™, which is a focusing drug that I am sure many know about. It is meant for ADD but can allow you to stay up real late. That is what I was using it for. On top of that, I was drinking a lot, dipping, and smoking. I was not in a good spot mentally, nor was I living as a good person in general.

This contradicted my upbringing because I was a missionary's kid. My parents were full of the Holy Spirit, had a mission in Mexico, and I witnessed miraculous stuff happen. They would do amazing things, but I did not know God at this time in my life. I had never had that moment where you get hit with the reality of God. When I got to college, I started questioning everything. Being a witness was not enough, and I decided I did not necessarily believe it. I was learning about all the chemicals in my brain, and my brain got above my heart. I thought I was smart, but I certainly was not.

One night, my girlfriend and I were arguing. Things were not going well, and she wanted me to change. I was determined that I would not change. I said some hurtful words, and she started crying and walked away. At that moment, I broke down. Nothing felt like it was working. I was not doing well in school and was not doing well in my relationship. I sat down on the couch and said, 'God, you better show me what's going on right now!' That was a dumb statement.

I remember as a child having the gift of being able to see in the Spirit. Meaning I could see the supernatural angels and demons as they were in the natural. I had a couple of demons that pestered me when I was younger that my parents could attest to. Here I was now with this ability, and I had suddenly asked God to show me what was going on. At that moment, God opened my eyes and pulled the curtain back to reveal the truth. God took off the filters and let me experience it because that is what I had asked for. I fell to the ground and saw two 'demons' that looked like black shadows who were just playing with my life. I could see them and feel the torment coming from them, and it oppressed me deeply.

I started going through deliverance right there on my living room floor. (If you don't know anything about deliverance, it is when a demon has a grip on your soul and is oppressing you in a certain area of your life, is expelled. The action happens when the demon is commanded to leave because of the authority of Jesus.)

I did not understand what was going on, and my girlfriend was the only one there. She was freaking out, so she called my dad and said, 'He is freaking out on the floor, convulsing and all this stuff, and I don't know what is going on.' It was two in the morning, and my dad had seen this before and knew exactly what was happening. My dad agreed to come over and told her to begin to pray the blood of Jesus over me until he got there. Somehow, Baylor and I made it to the bathroom, and as we sat there, she was praying over me. The torment started to worsen to the point that it felt like things were tearing at my face. It was awful. This was probably the darkest thing that has ever happened to me.

Finally, my dad got there and started praying and taking me through deliverance and declaring the blood of Jesus over me. At the moment, I did not know what was happening to me, but I knew that I needed it because whatever he was doing was helping. Eventually, I was able to get through this attack, and I could stand up. I went home with my dad that night, and he talked to me about the incident. He laid out what happened and what took place in the Spirit, but he could not figure out what had caused this to happen. I told him what had been going on and what I had asked God for. He said, 'Yep, God's real, and demons are too. There's a whole spiritual realm that you haven't even seen.'

To be honest, I was freaked out by this. Despite that fact, I could not help but try to find answers, which led me to start asking many people lots of questions. Over the next several weeks, I discovered the truth and reality of the spiritual battle going on in people's lives. Coming out of this deliverance victorious put the power of God in me that set me on fire for Him.

(It is ridiculous that many people do not understand what they are experiencing. God is there to take care of them, but they must ask for it. I have a heart for those who are bewildered and confused, just like I was, because they simply do not know what they are doing.)

My girlfriend became my wife, and we began going to church. One day she told me that she wanted to go to an extra class before church and since I did not want to take two cars, I decided to go with her. There, I found a tribe of people who believed in God's authenticity and power the same way I had come to know Him. This validated everything I had come to know was true and furthered my exciting pursuit of God and His tangible presence.

There is a new passion that can come when you allow God to get a hold of you, and you can truly comprehend that it is a real thing. It makes you never want to stop experiencing that feeling of love that comes from walking with God. With this love comes power over the darkness that you walk through in life, and you have the responsibility of using it and then sharing it with others. This can help them with the things they are going through. It's simply an amazing journey, and I'm ready for more."

~Matthew

One of the most beautiful characteristics of God is that he does not get offended by us easily. Piercing even through our anger and hate, there is not a place that God is unwilling to meet us with the most intensity and intentionality that I have ever experienced. Although He shows up when I am ready, He is in persistent pursuit of me the entire time. Occupying the lonely barstool that long sat empty beside me, He took up the place that I had saved as a dream that was one notch below what I wanted, yet one notch above what I had decided I deserved.

My Father sits, He listens, He loves, and He forgives. He is big enough to know every detail, and there is nothing that can surprise Him and no need to justify our pain. Without a word, He knows. This can be intimidating when so much of society bases our story's worth on its shock value. Our worth has been preordained and can never be erased. My God can handle my anger, and yet honor my prayer, and then love me back from the place of being bitter. There is nothing that can make Him fall off His throne.

This is an open battleground, and the prize is priceless. The victory is predestined, and His love is transparent. So, I stand up, suit up, and take the first step of the rest of my life. I stay consistent and persistent. I am looking through His eyes where mine deceive me and feel His heartbeat where mine has grown cold. Life will always have ups and downs, but with my eyes wide open and an awareness of Who I choose to put my faith in, I will become more than a conqueror. Life is a testimony. How will I choose to tell my story?

My Father sits, He listens, He loves, and He forgives. He is big enough to know every detail, and there is nothing that can surprise Him and no need to justify our pain.

CHAPTER THREE
THE GREAT PHYSICIAN

"He heals the brokenhearted and binds up their wounds."

Psalm 147:3 (NIV)

"And he said to her, "Daughter, your faith has made you well; go in peace and be healed of your disease."

Mark 5:34 (ESV)

"On hearing this, Jesus said to them, 'It is not the healthy who need a doctor, but the sick. I have not come to call the righteous, but sinners.'"

Mark 2: 17 (NIV)

"Behold, I will bring to it health and healing, and I will heal them and reveal to them an abundance of prosperity and security."

Jeremiah 33:6 (ESV)

God is sometimes described as the Great Physician, also known as Jehovah Rapha, the God who heals. As stated by City on a Hill, in an article called "He is Jehovah Rapha, and He's the God Who Heals,"[7] they say: *"In Exodus 15, God gives himself a new name: Jehovah Rapha. Jehovah was not a new name. Jehovah means 'The Existing One' or 'Lord' and suggests 'to become known.' Rapha was the new part. Rapha*

---

[7] (Antonucci 2018)

means 'to heal.' God let the Israelites know that He is the God who heals."

What He said is more substantial than that. It is not so much, "I am the God who heals," as it is, "Healing is what I am." In the Bible, almost every single story of God showing up in a situation, or Jesus entering the scene, was a situation where a person, a people, or land needed healing. As much as God is the God of creation, so also is He the God of restoration.

***

Christianity's most beautiful thing has nothing to do with law or religion; it is the tangible way God desires to be involved in our lives. Miracles, signs, and wonders are not just in the Bible for the awe and wonder of a good story. They are placed as a road map to the possibility of the impossible. Our next narrative comes from Chris, who asked to tell his story of how God showed up and showed off in his life in a big way.

"My story starts with me being raised in a single-parent home with my mom as our sole provider. We never went to church at all, ever. I started drinking at sixteen. Growing up in a college town, that is all we ever did. Later I moved to Amarillo, went into the military, got out of the military, and moved back to Amarillo. I knew something was missing, so I started going to church. I never really got into the church I attended. It was big, so I could hide in the back row, which made me comfortable. I could hear God's word occasionally, but I figured He could not touch me. However, I always knew there was something there.

I finally hit a dark time in my life where I was extremely depressed and constantly sick. I had to have four or five surgeries within three years because of an injury I received in the military. At that point, depression started taking over. I kept it all in, kept it hidden within the walls of our family. I started having blackouts, and they got so bad I would wake up from them and cut myself and not even realize it. I was placed in the Pavilion (a mental hospital in Amarillo), went through their programs, was released, then had to go back again. The second time in the Pavilion (either the first or second night), I felt such a peace come over me. It was hard to explain. It was like everything was being washed off of me.

When I was released a few days later, I found out my wife came clean about everything to my brother. He had called and asked what was going on because Holy Spirit was talking to him. My wife finally let it all go and told him everything. My brother pulled over on the side of the road on his way home from Albuquerque so he and my wife could pray for me. The same time they were praying for me was the same time I had felt the relief and the cleanliness washing over me at the Pavilion.

At the time, I had been on so many medications for high blood pressure, kidney stones, and the migraines I was experiencing three to four times a week, and I pretty much lived in the ER. After leaving the Pavilion for the second time and after my wife and brother prayed for me, I was off every single medication within twenty days, and was completely healed of all my ailments.

I was still unsure of what was taking place in and around me. My brother told me that God loved me, and I knew there was something there, so I started seeking Him. We began going to the River Church in Panhandle, TX. That *is when I met my dear friends, Bill and Kathy (prophetic pastors that were visiting from another church). They invited me to class one Sunday morning, and it was not like anything I expected. They started talking about praying in tongues, and I was unclear about their message. The funny thing was is that I had always spoken in a foreign tongue in my mind while lying in bed. I laughed at myself and wondered if I was part Cherokee or something because it did not sound right. Come to find out, it was my Heavenly Father talking to me the entire time I was broken. That was when I realized just how much the Father truly, genuinely loves everything. Ever since I have been seeking after Him, everything has all been on His time and schedule because He is always there for me."*

~Chris

God's original plan was for us to never experience sickness in any form. There were no walk-in clinics built into the garden of Eden or therapy sessions written into Adam and Eve's schedule. It was total freedom, that is still possible today, to be seen, be known, and to know in complete perfection. We are receiving love from our Creator and Father in a beautifully symbiotic way. He is the Potter, so we are fashioned as clay in the most wondrous and astonishing way. Think of the intricate way our bodies are knit together. Systems are functioning harmoniously; nerves are firing and responding in sync. The marvel with which our brains comprehend, remember, and connect with our hearts to create such complex emotions, we often don't know how to handle them. It seems to be much harder to imagine that something this beautiful could happen without the involvement of Someone greater than me.

Often, this can be explained with an illustration of a book. A book cannot create itself. With its cover and perfectly formed sentences, illustrations, and binding, it logically must have an author and/or publisher. DNA that makes life possible and is the foundational genetic material of creation is often called the "Book of Life." Scientifically, something cannot come from nothing, and thus, there must be a beginning that far outweighs our logic or reasoning. So much of our bodies are created to regenerate naturally. Bones, skin, blood cells, even the lining of our stomach and parts of our brain regenerate at different, but consistent rates. So, why do we get sick or even need healing? What happened and got in the way? It is because of sin, and as a bi-product, sickness.

Sin can develop and manifest either physically or mentally, and even more often, a combination of both. This manifestation is the work of satan trying to take out the one thing God cares about more than anything—you and I. Despite the twisted schemes of this fallen angel, God gave us a solution through Jesus Christ. In 1 Peter 2:24 (ESV), it says, *"He himself bore our sins in his body on the tree, that we might die to sin and live to righteousness. By his wounds, you have been healed."*

God had a solution to the sin issue from the moment it took place. His heart was so saturated with love for us He sent His only begotten Son to take on human form and be sacrificed in our place. It was not enough to simply die in our place; He defeated death by returning to life and ascending to Heaven to be seated with God. This is spoken past tense, as in it already is a done deal. Jesus, being fully man and fully God, chose to take on the full punishment of sin, which was death. If you were the only person on the planet, He would have made the sacrifice just for you. Stepping into the fullness of what Jesus offers us defies all human logic and seems impossible. Yet, by who's logic do we deem it impossible? When we trust what Jesus did for us and truly accept Him as our Lord and Savior, there is an undeniable shift.

In this place of calling Jesus to dwell in us, it equips us with the power, love, and authority He demonstrated while here on Earth. Faith and familiarity with God are the secret combinations that allow this tangible authenticity to grow. In John 14:12, Jesus speaks to the disciples a truth still viable today. *"Very truly I tell you, whoever believes in me will do the works I have been doing, and they will do even greater things than these, because I am going to the Father."* That is absolutely astounding to ponder. The miracles, signs, and wonders that Jesus displayed were beyond comprehension, and here He declares that *they* will do even greater things. Who is this *they*? *They* are not merely the disciples but *anyone* who believes.

Healing comes to people mostly through others who pray and/or lay hands on a person. There is something beautiful in the way that God loves to use people to bring healing. With the humble prayer of desperation, seeking His goodness, or even distant skepticism, the Creator can meet us and use it all. When we read the Bible, while none of them are explained the same way, many of Jesus' miracles are described as a training manual for how to start stepping into the *greater things.*

In the fifth chapter of the Gospel of John, a man was lying at a healing pool.[8] When Jesus came to the man, he had an infirmity that kept him from receiving healing. Jesus asked

---

[8] (BibleGateway n.d.)

him if he *wanted* to be healed, not if he deserved to be there, not what he would do if healed, not if he wanted the attention of it, just if he *wanted* it. He had an apparent need for physical healing but still had to step into the reality of his situation and condition, then step into obedience, truth, and trust. When the man responded by faith, he was instantly healed and could get up and walk. A victory resulted because his excuses were put away, and he decided to believe in Jesus more.

A woman at a well in John 4 was emotionally sick.[9] Her worth had been as depleted as the previous man's infirmity. Jesus met her on the way to His original destination because He is always willing to take time for the one. She was dehydrated in her spirit and hung up on religious theology and political correctness. There was a burden of shame from her past, and her current sin kept her captive. Jesus simply spoke her truth to her in love. The conviction and reality of Who was speaking to her created a transformation. There was an invitation extended to believe, and because of faith, she was transformed. She was healed, not from a physical ailment, but heart and soul issues. The conviction of the truth Jesus spoke was so wrapped in love that what was once hidden became a testimony of freedom.

*****

God created us and knitted us together in our mothers' womb, which means He knew and loved us first. He is always for us and desires good things for us. Sometimes miracles happen because of faith, and sometimes they occur as an appointment to meet the One in whom our faith lies.

---

[9] (BibleGateway n.d.)

Healing is not just for the body, but also the soul, spirit, and unhealthy mindsets, because God's heart is to see us wholly restored. The next individual hitting these pages with their powerful account can authenticate this truth. Kasey's world was radically rocked because of a miraculous healing that took place in her life. Even with this event's magnitude, it was simply an invitation to step into a new level of complete restoration.

"When Jon and I got married, we had a radical experience with God. Before that, we would go to church, say a little prayer, and keep going on as usual. We were living together at the time but not married. The Lord slowly started convicting us as we were going to church, but did so in such a sweet way. An ultimatum was given to both of us by God at separate times, 'Get married or separate.' Neither one of us wanted to get married because we were young, so it sounded crazy. We realized we wanted to do the right thing, no matter what. With this mindset, we called our pastor and got married on our lunch break. We eloped from the prompting of the Lord. One of the things that God showed me during that time was that it was not about the wedding; it was about marriage. We would eventually have a vow renewal service, which was such a special thing since we never had a traditional wedding.

Unfortunately, shortly after we got married, I had a miscarriage. I went to the doctor, and he told me that I had many issues, and I may never have children. From the time I was ten until I was about thirteen years old, I had been abused by my stepdad. The abuse caused irreversible damage that would make the process of having kids impossible. I simply decided I did not receive that.

When we got married, Jon and I dedicated all we had and all we were to God. 'All-in' was not just a term for us. We removed every album we had, cleansed every outside influence, we even got rid of our TV. That might not be necessary for everyone, but we both came from such toxic environments we needed a radical transformation. God needed us to be in that space of total abandonment so that He could do the necessary work in us.

At one point, a guy began coming every night to speak at our church. There was radical, charismatic worship and ministry that lasted up to four hours. As hungry baby Christians, we just wanted more and more of all that God had for us. We were going to church every night. One night during this time, my medical issue came to my mind. I simply told the Lord, 'Lord, this was not my sin. I believe that you're going to heal me.' I mentioned to Jon, 'I'm not saying that we're going to have kids right away, but I'm asking for God to heal me.' His eyes got huge in a way that showed shock, but he also said, 'Okay.'

A short time later, the service was finishing, and everyone was just kind of hanging out. As the worship died down, we were sitting at the altar and hanging out on the stairs when the evangelist got up from his seat. He went to the microphone and said, 'God is healing some of these women right now.' Instantly, I got such a pain in my stomach that caused me to double over, grab Jon's leg, and squeeze it. I then heard the words, 'You are healed!' echo in my heart. Looking up at Jon, I told him that the Lord just healed me. Being bold, Jon walked up to the speaker afterward and told him that I received the healing tonight. To everyone's surprise, the speaker responded, 'Well, congratulations, Daddy!'

Two weeks later, I was pregnant with our oldest daughter. That was when I truly believed that God listens. He hears me, and He cares. He is involved in every part of our life. This whole experience propelled me forward in my faith. (The amazing thing about faith and relationship with our Heavenly Father is the grace that comes with it.) While this miracle was life-changing, it did not fix everything. While it spoke love to me, I did not fully understand it at the time.

I always had 'daddy issues' because my dad was not a good dad (my biological dad, that is). He is a good guy, but he was not a good dad. Part of the reason was that he was a young dad and just not involved. It took me a long time to get to a place where I walked in the Father's love. I never felt like I had a father's love, so I did not know how to soften my heart to receive that sentiment. Fast-forward more than 15 years when I fully realized God's love. (I know it sounds like a long time, but it was a process for me.) When that powerful, beautiful love broke through the walls and barriers I had built, it was an irreversible, perfect moment.

The motto of our life is 'grace upon grace' because the Lord has been so gracious to us. He gives us the time we need to heal and grow in our understanding of Him. No matter where we feel there is a lack, God is there with the wisdom needed to succeed. God gave us a scripture in 1 John 2:27, 'As for you, the anointing you received from Him remains in you, and you do not need anyone to teach you. But as His anointing teaches you about all things and as that anointing is real, not counterfeit- just as it has taught you, remain in Him.'

Summed up, it means that you do not need a man to teach you because Holy Spirit will teach you all things. It had been another longing for our lives, a desire of our heart to have a spiritual mother and father to mentor us and lead us. The Lord was so good in not allowing that because it forced us to press into His wisdom and heart and truly know Him as Father.

There has been so much confirmation along the way. For example, we have heard messages and words of insight preached from pastors and different speakers that we already knew. We never heard it from a person, but were taught by God. As a good Father stewarding us, He would reveal supernatural understanding. This encouraged us to learn to hear Him and obey Him through our lives.

There has been such a transformation through His grace. Statistically, considering our siblings and family, we should not be where we are. Nevertheless, the grace of God transcends statistics. Us being willing to obey and listen to Him allowed Him to walk us through the process, because He is so Fatherly. I know now, He knew we were not ready to deal with some things, so He did not deal with it. He simply let us walk until we were ready for healing and change. It took us a long time to get to a place of wholeness and healing.

We do not feel like there is a time when you fully 'arrive.' Things still come up, and God is still gracious with us, but we are a lot further ahead than we once were. There are habits, mindsets, relationships, and strongholds that you will stay blind to in ignorant bliss until you are ready to deal with them. God will never throw anything in our face demanding we deal with it immediately. He is so Fatherly and so Gracious so that we can handle the course correction.

When it was time, and we were ready, He would give me a dream. As I slept, it was like Father spoke right to me, and I woke up and knew exactly what to do. Questions like, 'What do I do with this?', or 'How do I deal with that?' Walking us into wholeness, our Heavenly Father was a gracious and good Father. When God comes in as the Great Physician to heal, He does a full system sweep of everything that needs a touch. From physical wellness to the cleansing and rehabilitation of our soul, He is up to the task and willing to be as patient as necessary to get the job done."

~Kacey

All life comes from our Creator, and He is not concerned about the limitations we believe prevent us from seeing things happening. Before the beginning of time, knit together in our mothers' wombs by our Heavenly Father, we were accepted and predestined for such a time as this. We were not knit by our mother, nor knit by generational curses, rejection, or evolution. Our Father did the creating that brought us into this world. When I became born again or 'saved,' it meant I had been re-fathered by the best Dad ever. Salvation is amazing because it creates the Spirit of Adoption that allows us space to be known and to know our new Dad. Immediately, I was grafted into the Kingdom as a child of God.

In direct contrast, we walk as orphans outside of this place, and everyone feels like our problem. We are highly emotional and broken, so we go to therapists and psychologists to answer our rejection issues. This need for answers stems from us being logical people who have a desperation to *know*. Unfortunately, as we saw from Adam and Eve's example, sometimes knowing will bind you and make you more of a prisoner, rather than setting you free. If we allow Holy Spirit to lead us, we learn it is more important to know what has been made right rather than wrong.

As difficult as it is to swallow, I was my problem, and you are/were your problem. I am not referring to authentic moments of victimization, but instead to the more profound spiritual peace we all seek. Someone may mistreat me, reject me, steal from me, or take me for granted, but I have the power over how I will react. There is a basic understanding that life will not always be "fair," but I get to choose who I will be in each trial.

Good news, though, when I got born again, I was set free. I finally saw my created value and did not need the approval of others. As stated in Ephesians 2, we are accepted and beloved.[10] No one can take away the acceptance that God gave me. Not my mom, not my dad, not that coworker who conspired against me, not that religious leader who left me lost and hurt, and certainly not the college boy who molested me. Rejection cannot stay with me unless I give it a place to habituate.

On the contrary, I should become so convinced God means what He says—that I am covered in His pure, true love. This love does not promise everyone will like me, but it does fill me with the grace not to care. This love empowers me to handle anything that comes my way with honor, dignity, and wisdom. This love *never fails*!

My Child,

You walk through life feeling like it is all flying past you, just out of reach. You feel so temporary, so insignificant,

---

[10] (BibleGateway n.d.)

asking the question, "What is the meaning of it all?" I watch you seeking out temporary explanations to permanent problems. You dilute pain, helplessness, depression, loneliness, and anger with solutions from the world.

You may be at a point of giving up all hope because it seems like hope is a fantasy. In your heart, mind, body, spirit, and soul, it feels like every piece of you has been in a battle to survive. Walls have been built to protect you, but these walls are suffocating. Like shackles and chains, you feel restrained and hindered from something better, something more.

However, you no longer dream about what that something more could possibly be. A very present enemy is seeping into your place of safety and poisoning you. The lies he whispers intensify the negative and draw you further and further from the positive. The sickness the enemy brings engulfs you and makes you feel incapacitated. Every step feels heavy; every day, even every breath seems like it requires more effort than the day before. This brings an increased need for solutions, relief, and answers. Most of this relief comes from all the wrong places, but it seems justified because "that's just life," right?

It does not have to be. This does not have to be your reality. There is a final answer. Love is this answer. Love heals all. Love cries out to you now. Love calls your name. I AM Love. I am the God of all gods, the Lord of all lords, the King of all kings, and the greatest of all physicians. I can heal all, and I sent the perfect solution to all problems—the perfect solution to all sickness.

I sent the perfect manifestation of My love, and His name is Jesus. My precious, beloved, and flawless Son removes the gap that separated My precious children from their Heavenly Father. You are My beloved child. I saw every imperfection, every sin, and Jesus washed it all away, past, present, and future. It is not too good to be true. Believe this truth with all your heart. I am totally and radically in love with you, and I seek a relationship with you, every piece of you. I am the Doctor of all doctors because I can heal all that ails you. You can come as you are, but you will leave radically transformed.

I formed you, planned you, created you, molded you, and shaped every piece of you, from personality to smile. I see you, the original model, and it is exceptional. I will restore health to you and heal you of your wounds. Your heart is a different matter. I am a master heart surgeon, and when you decide to trust Me, I will give you a brand-new heart, a heart that has the Kingdom as its frequency and beats to the rhythm of My will.

Be reconciled to Me. My child, I implore you, let Me rewire your internal hard drives so that we can be compatible once again. I have the greatest anti-venom to satan's poison, and it is Christ. He represents My tangible love, full of grace, peace, and truth. It may seem too good to be true, but I am the God of impossibilities. I am the God of miracles, the God of creation from beginning to end. I am the God who causes the lame to walk and the dead to be raised. I am the God who can part the sea and save the wicked from the clutches of darkness.

I can take a dry and desolate wasteland full of drought and death and pour into it rivers of life—the rain and water of nourishment and sustainability. Let Me do this for you. Allow My presence to fill you, My goodness wash over you,

My grace to pour down on you, and My love to smash through every dam you have built up over the years, hoping to protect yourself.

Do not hesitate or be afraid, for you are stepping into the most exciting experience of your life. I want only good for those I seek a relationship with, and with all My heart, I pursue you. Your heart will beat steady and true as the old is replaced with the new. Your lungs will breathe in a deep new life as the heaviness that once sat on your chest is lifted. From your mind, I will raise the fog of indecision and hopelessness, and they shall be replaced with wisdom and joy. Loneliness is banished, for I will never leave you. Depression is banished, for my hope is permanent. Fear and anxiety may have bound you, but today, in Jesus' name, you are set free; the binding falls to the floor, powerless to hold you back.

I may not be the solution you are searching for, but I am the solution you need. I may not have been your first choice, but I will be your last choice, your final answer, and the right choice. There is nothing, not one tragedy, one hurt, one disappointment or trial that I cannot use for My glory. I am the ultimate optimist. I do not merely see the glass as half-full, but overflowing with mercy and love. I do not see rainbows after storms; I create promises that cannot be destroyed. I do not wish on stars, but I create tangible dreams you can step into and walk out your fantasies.

Look at everything as I do, as I transform the lens through which you look at life. Your scars will become your badges of honor. You will tell others of how I healed you and, in turn, bring healing to others. You thought that the world was hardening you, closing you down, and shutting you off from becoming something great. That was a picture painted by satan with lies. You are My greatest weapon, forged in the fire of life, heated, and strengthened for a specific purpose. In the areas you felt defeated, you are now stronger and wiser. Let Me take all the broken mess and restore, remold, and reshape this into something beautiful, like a Phoenix rising from the ashes.

Take action to step into who I created you to be. Have faith, son or daughter, that you can do all things through Christ who strengthens you. Like physical therapy for the soul, not everything I ask of you will be easy, but it will give you some of the most significant breakthroughs of your life, even as anger and hate try to creep in. For those who have hurt you, you must do the most challenging thing you will ever do, and forgive them. Release yourself from the snare that kept you tied down. Release yourself from the torment of hate and place it in My hands. You are not accepting their actions, words, or behavior. You are not saying what they did was okay or acceptable. You are simply allowing Me to be the judge as you faithfully step into the role of disciple. You are trusting Me with not just the good, but with every little piece of you. The pieces which are the hardest to let go of will bring the greatest breakthrough. As I heal you, you will not forget all the pain, but you will be able to feel empowered in the places you initially were defeated. You will be a warrior for the wounded and a light on a path of rescue for those trying to wander away from the darkness.

It is in My nature to love, and it is supernaturally effective. This love has the ability for transformation to spring from everything it touches. Know Me through our relationship. Learn My nature, get to know Me, not as a stranger, but as your Father. Know that when you cry out to Me, you can hear My voice and respond.

Be healed and walk every day as a testimony of what I can do. Walk every day, knowing I am for you, not against you. Remember, through experiences with me, confirmations, not coincidences, how personal and intimate My relationship with you is. Open your eyes and see. May the fog lift and the scales fall away, so you can see what you have been missing. May your ears open, and your heart melt to the truth of My pursuit and love for you. You are my favorite.

I will transform your scars into something beautiful. You are a mosaic masterpiece, a stained-glass wonder sealed with pure gold. You will shine as My light shines through you, your story, and your tests. A puzzle that seemed to be missing the essential piece, Jesus, becomes complete as you cling to Me.

Your strength will increase, your voice will find authority, and you will walk with the confidence you never thought possible. I did not send My Son for just the healthy; I sent the ultimate answer for the sick. So, come to Me, all who seek relief, and I will give you rest. My love is enough; it is the ultimate prescription. All you must do is be faithful to reach out and take it. You are My incredible creation; realize Who you belong to and step into that identity. Welcome home, My child.

My love is always with you, for I am still with you. I see you. I love you!

Your Great Physician, your Master Heart Surgeon, your God, your Abba, your Biggest Fan

CHAPTER FOUR
EXCHANGE OF COURAGE

Many times, we spend our time looking through the darkened prism of hope, shadows of disappointment blocking the brilliance of uncharted dreams. We cling to the ashes as they slip through our fingers, impossible to put back together with the glory of our original vision. This leaves disappointment to breed discouragement and leads us to the lonely, disheartened corner. We stop, and we sit in this place until the tugging on our heart becomes unbearable and causes our feet to move again. Perhaps part of this tug caused you to pick up this book.

As we press through this disappointment, the failure to fulfill the hopes or expectations that we created for ourselves lining the hallways of our mind, we begin to change the perspectives of what prevented our hopes or expectations from being realized. As we loosen our grip on the limited vantage point from which we take life in, we find the *appointment* that God has predestined for us. As His Spirit reaches, He draws out our sin and brings us to an intimate relationship with Himself. He whispers the words you have desired to hear for so long, but previously muffled ears could not hear. When your head is underwater in a sea of being overwhelmed, there is no way to position yourself to see what God sees, hear what He hears, or be what we were designed to be.

Thank You, Jesus, You call us out of this water! Thank You, Jesus, that being in this place is a choice! Thank You, Jesus, this is not our permanent residence! As we stand in the doorway of prospect, we have a choice. We can make this appointment and trade in our *discouragement* for the courage that only comes from God. He allows us to trade in our disheartened spirits for a newly transformed heart. We can stare at our circumstances with only failure as the outcome, *or* we can stand with victory as our final answer. No matter how dark or dismal the surroundings, we can know that there is a light around that corner. Even as I walk through the valley of the shadow of death, I have the opportunity to fear no evil! Not because I am brave, not because I am good enough, not because I have what it takes, but because God walks *with* me.

This is not my place to stop, to take it easy, or to take a pause. No, *this* is my place to keep going, keep pushing, and keep moving forward. There *is* something better up ahead. My Heavenly Father does not leave me to walk in this place alone. He is ever beside me, ever-present, ever-encouraging, and ever-loving me through His Holy Spirit. When I reach the place where it all becomes too much, He carries me. My tangible, relational God lets me fall back into His arms and continues to push me forward as I rest in Him. In His name, I come alive, for His name is Victory. He can illustrate hopes and expectations with a brilliance that far outweighs what we had planned in this backdrop of darkness. This place of "nothing to lose" is the place that the impossible can become possible as we trust in Him.

God is not afraid of my questions. It is in this interview of trying to understand that He can reveal His nature to me. If I do not seek, I shall never find. In the trials of life, we can truly see the essence of an individual. The same goes for the King of all kings and my relationship with the Creator of the universe. It is in this place that we see what our Father God is made of and what He can do. He *draws us into* that which He created us for. As we experience an authentic relationship with Him, we step out of the place of blind faith and into an irreversible trust, unmeasurable love, and into a *hope* that we cannot be talked out of. In a place that all that could previously be heard was "cannot," "will not happen," or the cynical pressing into nothing, we can now replace with a confident and mighty "but God!"

The Alpha and Omega eradicates all fear, and He puts a new light in our mind's eye. The God Almighty is not in the business of *not*. He is in the business of *yes and amen*! The Great I Am is in the business of *abundance*! Yahweh is in the business of *blessings* and *triumph*! Christ is our currency that will cover the debt of sin. Allow yourself to make the exchange and let in the power of the incredible flood of His goodness.

There is nothing average about a life lived incorporating the ultimate power of Holy Spirit. It is not for the faint of heart! It truly is the most incredible adrenaline rush of your life. It is not a special bonus for the spiritual elite; it is for everyone. This is for *you*! You do not have to be "ready;" you just have to be willing. Are you comfortable sitting as a larva in your Father's hand, or is it time to find the courage to liquidate the average and fly into the extraordinary? Do you dare to be above average?

***

I now introduce one of my most precious friends. We first met as I came stumbling out of my darkness. I was seeking authentic friendships in a group at my church because I knew that without finding a community with others who were also trying to better themselves, I would not survive. It was here I met some of the most beautiful people I have ever known. We all had powerful testimonies and sought the Lord with all our hearts in the best way we knew how. Now my friend goes into prisons and gives hope to hopeless situations since he was also once lost but now found. Here is Ty's "coming to Jesus moment."

"I did my first shot of methamphetamines when I was sixteen-years-old and had already been drinking before that. As a kid, I started going to church at a local Baptist church with my mom. Regrettably, that went away whenever my mom and dad separated. Sunday became my time with my dad. Since my dad owned a bar, we hung out at the bar often.

After high school, I started bartending, and my alcoholism, addiction, and everything negative just took over my life. I was getting paid to party, so partying became my life for about twenty years. Eventually, I ended up on probation for possession, and two years into probation, I got my third DWI. Consequently, they revoked my probation and sent me to prison. I was waiting to go to SAFP (Substance Abuse Felony Punishment Facility) and was temporarily being held in the Randall County jail for three months. To pass the time, I read the Bible all the way through.

I have always thought about how I wish I would have studied the Bible until I talked to someone else about it. That is when it dawned on me that if I had studied it, I would not have received the powerful revelation I did.

I read in Isaiah around the first part of February 2006, and everything changed. It said, 'I will not accuse them forever, nor will I always be angry, then they would faint away because of me - the very people I've created. I was enraged by their sinful greed; I punished them, and I hid my face in anger, yet they kept on the willful ways. I have seen their ways, but I will heal them; I will guide them and restore comfort to Israel's mourners.' (Isaiah 57:16 -18)

I always thought of God as mean and angry. I was probably agnostic at the time, though I did not even really know what agnostic meant. I believed that there was something out there; I just did not pursue it in any way. I was too busy doing my own thing.

At that moment, I saw God as sad and tormented by what I was doing. Nevertheless, whenever I read the scripture, it was the first time I knew in my heart that there was a God that loved me. It was not a fearful thing. It was not somebody browbeating me or saying I would go to hell if I did this or that, or did not change my ways. It was pure love!

Whenever the Word said, 'I will heal them,' God told me this was the start of an exceptionally long journey. On my birthday in 2005, I went to court and got sent to prison. God did not save me from the consequences of my actions, but this time left me transformed. I still had many issues to deal with, I still had anger, I still had questions, but I was different. Every day, I was giving my tray of food away - breakfast, lunch, and dinner. I was even giving away all my commissary. Not because I did not have a use for it, but I needed to show these guys that there was something else, something better. There were already prayer circles I got involved in, but this was even bigger than just 'jailhouse religion.' This was just the beginning of something greater.

Since then, there are many other things that God has put in my life that have been so tangible, such as levels of relationship with the Creator of the universe that I did not know were possible. I knew God existed, and I knew He loved me unconditionally without a doubt. Still, the levels of love have increased, especially over the last two years. They have expanded exponentially to levels of love I did not even know existed. This love keeps getting stronger and more prominent. It's the most beautiful thing I've ever experienced, and it doesn't stop; it just keeps on going."

~Ty

Perfect love drives out all fear. The Bible encourages us to "fear not" 365 times.[11] Once for every day of the year, perhaps because God knew we would be challenged with moments of anxiety more than anything else. God's not trying to be controlling or condemning by instructing us not to fear. Instead, He is reminding us where our power lies. When we get consumed by fear, we become a prisoner to it. Perhaps this is why it is called a panic attack or anxiety attack. All reasoning, logic, and wisdom leave when circumstances shift to a place of fear.

Nonetheless, God never tells us to walk something out without giving us the ability to do so, or the steps to implement it. The most basic root of fear, no matter what the scenario it is presenting itself, is a loss of control. This shift into feeling powerless creates high distress levels as an impulse that tells us something is not normal.

The antonyms of fear are calmness and confidence. The most significant exchange of courage comes from releasing all the baggage, anxiety, and worry into God's hands. Father God gives us complete access to the fullness of everything He has

---

[11] (Galtiere n.d.)

to offer. He is in the business of solutions, not problems, and helps us shift into a place of walking out the solutions, as my friend has done, with total bravery. As Brené Brown says continually in her book, we must "dare greatly."[12] Sometimes daring greatly simply means trusting God in moments that our greatest tendency would be to fear.

***

We all know that fear can affect us physically as well as mentally. No one I have ever met knows that more tangibly than the next testimony to bolster this book's pages. Erin truly embodies the definition of an overcomer, and I am thrilled to get to share her story with you.

"I am an Optometrist and have been practicing for twelve years so far. Ironically, my mom has severe glaucoma. In the twelve years that I have been practicing, and with all the patients I have treated for glaucoma, she is an example of my worst-case scenario. She progressed extremely rapidly, and the truth is, she is going blind.

From this truth of her blindness, fear began to grow deep in me because I knew so much of the disease is genetic. I began telling myself, 'I am going to go blind.' I was so fearful that I did a test on myself when it all first began three years ago. The results did not say that I was going blind, but it did show that there was a possibility of that eventually happening. It really wasn't anything severe, but that possibility was all it took to create a debilitating fear in me that I was going to go blind.

---

[12] (May 2012)

No matter how I tried to justify it or ignore it, this became who I was; this fear became my identity in my subconscious.

The fear became so overwhelming that I began seeing shocking physical changes. I started losing my hair, developed hypothyroidism, as well as anxiety almost immediately. I did not understand what was happening. I had never had a health problem in my life, and yet, as you will see, I became a melting pot of mysterious issues.

Anxiety took over my life. It consumed my every moment. Sleep became impossible at night. I was waking up physically paralyzed with my limbs so dead asleep that I was in anguish. I could not fully wake up, nor could I move my body. I was simply stuck in a frightening limbo. The pain was so horrible that it eventually took over all aspects of my life, and I could barely move. Basic, everyday tasks like washing my hair became impossible. A weakness developed in my legs, to the extent that I would trip downstairs or be unable to move. Even breathing became extremely difficult. As these symptoms progressed, I developed tremors in my head, body, and all over my face. No matter what I did, they were impossible to control or stop. The tremors became my new normal, the only constant I knew.

It was impossible for even doctors to find the root of the problem. They were able to resolve the hyperthyroidism, but when they tried to treat the anxiety, they could not get ahold of it. I had recently given birth to my fourth son, so I was not even in a physical place yet where I could start working out as a means to combat the attacks. All the symptoms and stresses continued to build.

I remember a significant event when I visited Vegas for my first time on a work trip. While in the hotel room, because of my constant exhaustion, I fell asleep around late afternoon. While asleep, I had a nightmare. The whole dream was about Satan coming after me. I was trapped in an abandoned building, and he was equipped with a big toolbox. In this terrifying box of death, there was every kind of mystical tool designed to completely tear me apart. The plan was the obliteration of every system in my body, from top to bottom, until I was dead. I was trapped in this dream and could not escape from it. The terror finally woke me up as I screamed aloud.

I jumped up and threw open the curtains, attempting to catch my breath. Shining back at me through that open window was a beaming rainbow. As I stood there in shock, the Lord said, 'I promise. You have my promise; you will not die!'

That took place in October. Three weeks later, I got strep, but I did not get a sore throat or show common symptoms, so I did not know it at the time. Consequently, I became extremely sick. This went on so long; I developed sepsis. (This is where the infection from a common virus gets into your bloodstream and kills you if left untreated.) I knew I was septic, so I went to the doctor, who immediately sent me to the emergency room. When I was seen in the emergency room, they did not think that I could really be septic because it normally only happens in older patients. I was told, 'You're young and healthy, here's some medication, and you can go home.' That night I nearly died.

I ended up in the ER again, not remembering anything about it, really. I had to have emergency surgery and almost lost my life. They had to do a radical hysterectomy and scrub my insides because there was so much infection where the strep had manifested. I was in ICU for four days and in the hospital for a total of ten days. Every single part of my entire body had been infected, from head to toe, and every system attempted to shut down. With the severity of my case, it took so much to recover just from the sepsis alone. My body was struggling to recuperate from the hysterectomy as well. There was a tremendous hormone shift that suddenly caused my body to react intensely. With this combination, I had a multitude of problems. I had kidney stones, hair loss, had trouble seeing, and I could not walk because my muscles atrophied. The tremors were horrible, and pain took over every system. It became like a revolving door with the doctor, getting CAT scans, MRIs, X-rays, CTs, but despite all this, no one could figure out what was wrong with me.

During this time, several family members were taking turns staying with me and taking care of my four boys, and I happened to be by myself in the room. There was a moment between shifts that felt a presence. I looked up, and in the corner of my hospital room was the Angel of Death. I immediately said, 'No! You promised, Lord! You promised!' I was so weak I could not pray or do anything. I simply remembered that rainbow from the hotel room in Vegas and held onto the promise He gave me that day. Eventually, I was released from the hospital. They said I was 'free,' and I was 'good,' but that's when I truly had to start walking out the healing process.

The doctors really did not know what to do with me. I was supposed to be recovering and getting stronger, but I was not. My hair fell out, causing me to have to wear a wig.

I was using eye drops to prevent glaucoma that turned my green eyes brown. As a woman, these things just rocked my whole identity. I just felt like I was not me anymore and wondered, 'Where do I belong?' This led to a series of depression and anxiety medications. Every medication would work for a little bit, but then the symptoms and the tremors would come back. I discovered later that I had developed Post Traumatic Stress Disorder (PTSD) from the fear. Now, I was fearful of my kids and so many unusual things. There were so many lingering symptoms from the sepsis. Nobody talks to you about sepsis because it does not happen to young people. I was continually hearing, 'You're young, you're healthy, you're fine, and you'll recover.'

One night, I was sitting on my couch, crying out to God to heal me. I was claiming the scriptures He had given me, but I needed a tangible hope. At that moment, I cried out to Holy Spirit, 'If you want me to be healed, give me a sign.' Suddenly, I felt like a 'whoosh' over my whole body, and just like that, the tremors instantly stopped. For the first time in two years, I felt unquestionable peace throughout my body. It only lasted about ten seconds but long enough to know that God said, 'I will heal you. This is my promise to you.' From that time forward, I kept declaring, 'You said Lord!'

For five months, I held on to this. I would get breadcrumbs of encouragement to pull me through. He would give me a prophetic word that said, 'You have been through everything in order to make you stronger.' Then another prophetic word came, saying, 'You are healed, and you are a healer.' Then another, 'I'm here to heal you and not leave you broken.' Despite these amazing words, I had to fight to believe them and cling to them with unwavering hope.

Fast forward to several months later. My husband and I went to a prophetic conference in Vacaville on raising children in a prophetic household. Dan McCollum, Kris Vallotton, and several other prominent prophetic voices were there. During our time there, one of the prophetic activities was drawing on a card. We had to illustrate how someone would get from a cliff on one side of the card to a cliff on the other side. How does this person get to the other side? For mine, I decided the person would just take a big running leap of faith, just like that.

The Lord instantly said, 'That word is for you. I want you to stop all your medications. I don't care what the doctor's say; this is what I say.' Now, this did not seem a realistic request because, at this point, I was addicted to my medication to the extent that I was popping pills almost every two hours. As I fell asleep that night, I had a dream where I had my watch on, and it started beeping to alert me. I looked down at it, and it read, 'You're healed!'

As if these two words were not enough, the following day at the conference, one of the speakers was talking and said, 'The Lord told someone to throw away all your medication. You are supposed to stop everything and throw away your pharmacy. Ha, ha, ha, maybe not, but maybe so?' I was shocked because it was so clearly meant for me. No one wanted me to do it, but I followed through anyway and threw them all away.

This was not an instantaneous miracle. I had to do the hard work of walking it out. The symptoms that I had been using the medication to treat became that much more real and raged against me. The week after we got back, I went to a chiropractor to try some natural treatments.

Unfortunately, it was too much and threw my system into overload, and I passed out and ended up knocked out with whiplash and no explanation as to what caused it. I knew then I finally had to face my biggest fear from the culmination of all this sickness and get tested for MS.

The MRI test for MS came back perfectly clear. I was struggling with whether what happened was anxiety or MS, because I had no idea the power anxiety could hold. In my head, there was no way fear could be the root of everything I had been going through. After the results came back, I heard the Lord say, 'I wanted this to happen because I know your brain, I know how it works. I know what it is you need to move forward because you were faithful and took the steps. This, my daughter, was just my confirmation of what I already told you. This is scientific proof of what I already did for you.'

Gradually, day by day, the tremors began going away until one day, they were totally gone. I felt like even though God had the power to heal me immediately, He wanted me to fight for it. I would have taken it for granted if I had been healed quickly. I felt my Father say, 'I wanted you to appreciate the journey and discover who I was through it all. I wanted you to press in to find My goodness in the storm.'

Since then, I have had three people in my exam room that have been set free of anxiety because the Lord had me share my story of healing. The funny part is that I had no connection with these people outside of work, and yet, their story of freedom has made it back to me to be celebrated.

God began to say, 'Your story is not about you anymore. Do more than just own the story because it is for you to share with others. Just as you have been healed, so you will heal. That which has been set free from you will set others free.' There are so many other people that need to know something other than what the doctor is telling them. Even though I am a doctor, I was called to be a different kind of doctor who heals souls.

I now fully understand that those who have gone through much will experience much. A powerful testimony creates influence and impact as a byproduct. I needed to get rid of the fear to fully embrace all God called me to be, and there was only one way for me to do it. Does everybody have to go through something that big? No, but God knew me and knew that unless it was big, I probably would not have gotten the picture.

Regardless, I conquered fear. When you've looked at death right in the face, when you've seen it in your body, felt it in your soul, and saw the literal spirit of death, but you overcame; you are a miracle. God has given you the resurrection power of life. I am called an overcomer by my Heavenly Father, and in this place, I walk free of anxiety. I am completely healed of all symptoms, and I was able to hang up the wig about two weeks ago. God Himself brought me through the trenches from death to life, so there is nothing left to fear. His love is too great and His goodness so noticeably on display."

~Erin

"Therefore I tell you, do not be anxious about your life, what you will eat or what you will drink, nor about your body, what you will put on. Is not life more than food, and the body more than clothing? Look at the birds of the air:

they neither sow nor reap nor gather into barns, and yet your heavenly Father feeds them. Are you not of more value than they? And which of you by being anxious can add a single hour to his span of life? And why are you anxious about clothing? Consider the lilies of the field, how they grow: they neither toil nor spin, yet I tell you, even Solomon in all his glory was not arrayed like one of these. But if God so clothes the grass of the field, which today is alive and tomorrow is thrown into the oven, will he not much more clothe you, O you of little faith? Therefore, do not be anxious, saying, 'What shall we eat?' or 'What shall we drink?' or 'What shall we wear?' For the Gentiles seek after all these things, and your heavenly Father knows that you need them all. But seek first the kingdom of God and his righteousness, and all these things will be added to you. 'Therefore, do not be anxious about tomorrow, for tomorrow will be anxious for itself. Sufficient for the day is its own trouble.'"

Matthew 6:25-34 (ESV)

The most significant exchange of courage comes from releasing all the baggage, anxiety, and worry into God's hands. Father God gives us complete access to the fullness of everything He has to offer.

CHAPTER FIVE
MAJOR COMPONENTS

"But God, being rich in mercy, because of the great love with which he loved us, even when we were dead in our trespasses, made us alive together with Christ—by grace you have been saved— and raised us up with him and seated us with him in the heavenly places in Christ Jesus, so that in the coming ages he might show the immeasurable riches of his grace in kindness toward us in Christ Jesus. For by grace, you have been saved through faith. And this is not your own doing; it is the gift of God, not a result of works, so that no one may boast."
Ephesians 2:4-9 (ESV)

God is like a Potter, and we are the clay He uses and creates as His masterpiece. Worth, value, significance, and merit are often words that we have a hard time attaching to ourselves in a healthy way, if at all. Mistakes and imperfections keep us locked in a place of devaluing ourselves. This is so dangerous because when we do this, we devalue God. By cheapening our worth, we insult the Creator's hands Who formed us. When our Heavenly Father created His children, He did so in His image, blessed them, and declared, "It is very good!"

God designed us to partner with Him in all things, including giving us authority and power to rule here on Earth. He illustrates this by giving Adam the charge to take part in the naming of all the animals. In addition, we were not created as robots programmed to autopilot and coast through life. No, God created us with a free will, creativity, and a flourishing imagination to paint a beautiful life on the canvas with Him. He wants us to live *with* Him and do life alongside Him. We were not designed to be alone. God wants to be there with us as we find our authentic selves and become the person He created us to be.

*****

Our next contributor shares her experience of finding out who she was meant to be in the arms of her perfect Creator.

"One of the most profound, life-changing moments in my life was in 2011. I had known the Lord as the Deliverer, and I had known Him in other different ways and names, but I did not know Him as a loved daughter. He had delivered me from depression and Bulimia, so I knew Him in that way, but there was still something missing. I was already prophesying along with other ministry work and knew that I could not do that and still carry this burden.

I started going to this life group called 'Lovers of His Presence.' The Lord took me, and the group would just kind of sit there and soak in holy meditation. I was kind of (and still can be) a little intense. I want to just get to the point of things and go on; therefore, this life group was out of my comfort zone. We had to sit there and wait for the Lord to talk to us.

It took me a long time to commit to doing that, but I felt the Lord's hand on it, so I continued to go. After some time, still, nothing was happening. I was worshiping, but I was not feeling the love of the Father. I finally told the Lord, 'I want you to speak to me in a way that you never have before.' Suddenly, He took me through this vision.

I started to see myself at six-years-old. I was carrying a huge, heavy rock that was bigger than my head. On this rock were written the words, 'self-hate.' I was carrying this at only six years old. I looked like a scruffy little kid coming up this mountain. Then, I saw Jesus at the top of the mountain. He came towards me and met me halfway. The Lord Jesus looked at me, and He said, 'You were never meant to carry that. Will you give it to me?' Remember, I am six-years-old in this vision, so I handed Him the rock. Once I handed it to Him, He picked me up in that child-size body and declared, 'You'll never have to carry that again.' I learned at that moment what it felt like to be loved. I was loved unconditionally. It was not because of my performance, because I was not throwing up from Bulimia anymore, nor because I was living a certain way, but simply because He loved me. I knew unwaveringly in that instant; there was a price paid for me.

It was undeniably profound for me. I sat, basically face-planted, for about an hour and a half and had this beautiful time with Jesus. I felt heat from my head, all over my back, and down to my toes (heat can be a prophetic sign of healing). In addition, I felt the love of the Father—what it feels like to be unconditionally, forever loved, and nothing that I could ever do could separate me from this feeling.

It was life-changing for me because it took me out of performance and into being a daughter of the Most High King, from operating out of a gift and into operating out of identity. My entire perspective shifted. Now I could love people in the purest form, from a completely, ravishingly adored and loved position.”

~Jennifer

I love the power that lies in the discovery of our identity. Identity means “the characteristics determining who or what a person or thing is.” My favorite definition, though, is “serving to establish who the holder, owner, or wearer is by bearing their name and often other details such as a signature.”[13] We can advertise who our Creator God is by stepping into the fullness of the potential He placed inside us. We give Him honor by shining bright our light of blessed assurance that He did a good work when He created us.

There was a time at work when I was just beginning my journey of hearing the Lord that I looked down at my tattered and worn shoes. I could see glimpses of socks through the painfully apparent holes. I let out a heavy sigh. I was tempted to be discouraged; I was a hard-working single mom, but I felt there were some days I could never seem to get ahead. The sacrifices seemed to be continuous and were draining, even though I knew it was worth it.

Then I shifted my thoughts and smiled as I thought of my energetic and passionate boy running into the school that morning, and I tried to refocus. Then the voice of my Heavenly Father broke in! I had to hide in my storage closet at work to frantically scribble the lifeline of encouragement, hope, and perspective that came roaring to life as He spoke.

“Look up, My daughter, for I see you right where you are. I see those discouraging moments, and I want to change

---

[13] (Oxford Lexico n.d.)

your perspective. Where you look at those shoes and see lack, I see fullness. Those shoes have carried you toward Me as you trusted that I am your provider. Those shoes are running with intentionality into a deeper relationship, full of purpose and splendor. Those shoes have memories, precious places I have taken you, people I have placed in your path, and things you have done only while in them. With the support inside them, I am giving you a new stance, a new level of confidence, healing to those broken places, and endurance to push through every obstacle and overcome every setback.

Holes would not be in these shoes if you had not done work in them; therefore, I see things accomplished! Perhaps they come from working with excellence and bring Me glory as you go into hour eighteen still standing, and still pushing. Maybe it was while you were washing your 7,000th dish as you clean up the kitchen from the meal that your son didn't like, but you fed him well, and this he will remember. These precious shoes are dirty because you are doing life, not staying stagnant. They contain the original feet that I created attached to My beautiful masterpiece of wonder, who was knit together in her mother's womb.

I see the lack, but I am here to fill you to overflowing with a new faith because I am your provider. You are not alone, and the love and passion necessary to cherish each step you take will consume you. Even in tattered shoes, there is joy in these moments. All is well, My daughter, for I am here!"

Stepping into a place of owning the greatness that the Lord placed inside us starts by genuinely believing it. Even the secular world understands the power of positive thinking. How much more sustainable will it be if we have the power of the Holy Spirit to back our self-affirmations? This concept transformed my parenting strategy and gave me a level of self-confidence that is unshakable. Without this holy boldness, I would never have healed to a strong enough place to champion the greatness of someone I had very few good thoughts of at the time.

The vastness of God's love is so all-encompassing that there is no one that He does not love. He can see the greatness in everyone despite their current circumstances. This means that even those individuals that we are convinced the world would be better off without, God is their Heavenly Father too, and He loves them purposefully. I will be completely honest; I had a tough time with this truth for a long time. My concept of "fairness" did not match what the Almighty Judge ordained. The beauty of His power of reconciliation came through in a very personal way.

To shorten an exceptionally long story, I ended up in my early 20's in a very unhealthy relationship. I lacked my own identity, deeply depleted in self-confidence and worth, along with being all alone in a new city, which made for a dangerous combination for me. While I was finding my way in my career as a pastry chef, I was losing myself relationally.

After many years in a controlling, emotionally abusive, and strained relationship, I finally found the strength to leave. Unfortunately, I left with many painful memories, a broken heart, and a nine-month-old son living in a foreign state with geographical restrictions based on child custody, which kept me trapped 1,600 miles away from my closest family. I had so much resentment and anger built toward this man I did not know how I could even look at him, let alone co-parent a child together. When I left the relationship, I began my slow recovery mission and began to rediscover God and heal from years of pain and self-deprecation.

The more I healed, the more forgiveness crept into my heart. I began to volunteer with a prison ministry focused on preventing recidivism through faith and reconciliation. As I left the prison celebrating the lives God was touching through me, I would think about my son's father and tell God, "Well, you can't get them all." Eventually, God softened my heart enough that I began to have the courage to pray for my ex.

One day as I was praying, I heard God say, "You should tell him to go to church." I enthusiastically agreed and was more than willing to pass that message on. Before I could pick up my phone, I heard the rest of the instructions. "You will invite him to your church, and he will sit next to you." "Uh, *hell no!*" was my immediate and forceful response. The very thought made my blood boil. I had carefully crafted a very safe new environment that he had never entered. I had new friends that did not know him and a place I called my second home, a place I did not want him welcomed.

God had different plans. After several weeks of fighting and arguing with God, I finally gave in and agreed to ask my ex because I was sure that he would say no. He responded, almost immediately, "Sure."

"CRAP!"

Now I was committed to a scenario I had no control over but was determined to go through with. My prayers went into overdrive.

The day arrived, he met me at church, and God showed up. That day I watched my son's father give his life to Christ. He then got water baptized and was baptized in the Holy Spirit shortly after. He changed in ways I never expected, and that could only be attributed to a God-sized miracle. He has had a huge breakthrough in his anger issues. Compromise and communication have significantly increased between us, and mutual respect has become imperative.

Today I can say we are a co-parenting miracle. We will never get back together, but we can keep God as the source of our wisdom and remember that it is about our son and not us. We have gone through some tough challenges with our son and have been able to navigate them through teamwork and grace. I have learned not to refer to him as "my baby's daddy" but to honor him as my son's father. While I may not always agree with his life decisions, my child has little need to know about my feelings. Half of every kids' genetic makeup comes from either parent. This means that if I insult one of those halves, my child will internalize those insults as there is something wrong with him. God's grace and love are for all His children, even the ones I do not get along with.

In hindsight, I do not know why I stayed with my ex as long as I did but, now I am so glad I did. I would not be where I am, who I am, or have the amazing son I do if I had not stayed. God can not only heal all things; He can transform the circumstances to accelerate us into everything we were meant to be. Healing is not merely physical but can integrate our body, soul, and spirit. Doe Zantamata says, "Anyone can hold a grudge, but it takes a person with character to forgive. When you forgive, you release yourself from a painful burden. Forgiveness does not mean what happened was OK, and it does not mean that person should still be welcome in your life.

It just means you have made peace with the pain and are ready to let it go".[14]

***

As we heal, we can set aside our feelings for God's will and be used powerfully. We could be the only way that someone will come to know Christ, so step into the freedom God has set before you and let freedom ring. Connie watched her circumstances transform before her very eyes as she stepped out of surviving life into thriving. God accelerated her into everything she was meant to be in a beautiful way.

"I grew up in a deeply religious home. My parents got saved when they were newly married and jumped right into a deeply charismatic church. Neither one of them grew up in the 'ideal' environment, and their parents did not raise them in godly homes. When they found God, they decided they wanted to raise their children differently and began to create the blueprints for what that would look like.

We grew up on a farm, about nine miles from the closest town and sixty miles from the nearest McDonalds. Out in the middle of nowhere, my parents did the best they could. They were extremely strict parents. We had excessive rules, including no dances, limited movies, and we didn't even own a TV. My siblings and I were not allowed to go anywhere but to church. Every time the doors were open, we were there.

When I was in fifth grade, we got pulled out from public school, and my three siblings and I were

---

[14] (Zantamata 2019)

homeschooled. We were at home all the time, isolated and secluded. My older sisters were in high school at the time and had cultivated a friend group that was hard for them to leave. On the other hand, I loved being pulled out of school because I was shy and was getting bullied. For me, this arrangement was a blessing.

Being raised in an extremely religious home, I had a great foundation instilled in me, but God was introduced and portrayed as a big scary God. I did not have a clear view of who God was. To me, He was just a bunch of rules. There was always the fear that if God happened to come back for the rapture, right after you had said a cuss word or something like that, then well, you weren't going to go to Heaven. You were going to miss it because of your slip up. This left me with an unhealthy fear and terror of God.

Working on the same team was Holy Spirit, Who was somebody that tattled on me. My dad would tell my sisters that he knew when they were doing something wrong because the Holy Spirit told him. I was very firmly planted in a works, 'strive to be good enough,' based religion.

I looked to my older sisters as beacons on how to navigate my life and what not to do most of the time. The oldest simply did what she had to do to get through high school without making too many waves. Shortly after graduating, she married her husband and moved away.

In direct contrast, my other sister Jessica was very rebellious, very headstrong, and very independent. She argued with my dad all the time while I stood in the background and witnessed it unfold. She and my dad were equally matched in that neither one was willing to lose. I remember fights that would start between them, that would last well into the night. I would be in bed long before they would stop their fighting and arguing.

I watched as my sister went through this cycle continuously. She would sneak out and do things that were certainly against the rules. Even though I always knew what she was up to, I never told on her because I hated the fighting. As I watched her go through all this, I decided I was not going to live that way. I fashioned myself to be the absolute best of the best. I never got into trouble. I did not even date anyone or even think about dating because I saw what happened with my sisters. Dating was the connection I made as to why my dad was so hard on them.

I finished my high school education through homeschool and then went off to college. I did not even know what I wanted to do; all I knew was that I did not want to stay in mom and dad's house forever. I was ready to leave. I decided to attend a Christian college because that is what I assumed was expected of me, and I was a people pleaser. I decided to be a children's pastor, even though it was not my desire. I did not enjoy working with children, but it is what I did at church. I wanted to do anything and everything to make my dad or mom proud. Most of all, I wanted to please my dad. He was the one that made the biggest deal about what we were doing, which determined if we were a good person and worthy of his time and attention.

I was constantly trying to gain approval from my dad. He was never the kind to say, 'I love you.' I could probably count on my hands when he said it. I was starved for his approval, so I worked excessively for just those few words confirming that I was doing good. Sticking with what

I knew, I just did everything I was supposed to do and continued going through life.

I met Jay (my now husband), my junior year. His family went to our church, and that is how we got to know them. We started as friends and then began to date a few years later. This irritated my dad. Jay's dad was so laid back and so easygoing, the opposite personality traits from my dad. My dad always assumed this dictated that the individual must be lazy. Consequently, he expected Jay was going to be a lazy guy as well.

Dating Jay was the first thing I ever did that went against my dad's wishes. He never came out and voiced his disapproval to me but preferred to share with my mom, who would then tell me. Honestly, being so starved for his approval, I probably would not have gone forward with Jay if he had been vocal about it.

Jay and I dated for two years, got married, and moved to Greenville, Texas. We floated through life, checking off the boxes of things you are supposed to do; get a job, have kids, go to church, live life one day at a time. We found a Baptist church to go to that had people I liked and were fun to be around. I was not doing anything wrong, but I was not getting closer to God. I was still really confused about who God was and what His role in my life was.

I doubted that God could even use me during this whole time because I did not have a 'story.' I did not have this elaborate encounter with God that saved me. I had heard speakers tell of how they used to be into drugs and alcohol, their life was a disaster, and then they would have a 'come to Jesus moment' when their eyes were opened, and they decided to turn their life around and serve God. It seemed that God used them in these huge ways because of the disaster they had overcome. I felt like I was on the back burner spiritually and that consistently being a good person was not good enough.

I went through times of just being frustrated. I knew that there had to be more to a relationship with God than what I had. Unfortunately, I did not know how to receive it or even how to handle the information that I had and known to be true. I became irritated with religion and even Christians. These people told me that I should be one way but then did not even live that way themselves. All these unanswered questions morphed into a bitterness that I carried for several years.

This came from the unhealthy hang-up I had involving Holy Spirit. I grew up believing that you were not filled with the Holy Spirit if you did not speak in tongues. Taking it a step further, it was questionable as to whether you were even saved or not based on that one aspect. If not, several individuals would surround you and pray for you forever. There was generally pushing and yelling, to the point it was terrifying. I had spent a large part of my childhood, at the altars of church camps, trying to receive the Holy Spirit. I clearly remember being on the floor at church, begging God to give me the gift of tongues so that I could be qualified. Having never received it as a kid, by the time I was an adult, I had stopped even worrying. Faking speaking in tongues just became a habit to not attract attention.

In the meantime, Jay and I moved, and when looking for churches, I picked a huge church I could go to on Sunday morning, check the box on my imaginary, 'I am a good kid chart,' not have to be accountable to anybody and basically hide. We stayed invisible for around seven or eight years, just running around that circle. We were doing life, but not actually living.

Finally, we decided to go to a life group but just randomly picked one. I do not even know why we chose it. At the time, neither one of us drank coffee, yet the group was called 'Coffee Club.' We met another couple there we clicked with right away. When we got to know them a little bit, they kept talking about something called 'discovery classes.' I was not interested at all. It didn't sound enjoyable to me. The only one that remotely piqued my interest was 'Discover Holy Spirit,' but that came from my issues with Holy Spirit as a child.

Eventually, Jay decided to go to these discovery classes and would come home with stories of incredible encounters with God—encounters with people hearing God's voice so clearly that there was an understanding that was changing his mindset of who God was. It was creating a healthier mindset that included a totally foreign concept to me called grace. While he would tell me how incredible it was, he would also talk about having to get up and speak to people. Me, being my shy self, decided that could never be me. I did not want to speak to two or three strangers, let alone get up and say anything in front of a whole room full of people.

Eventually, I caved and joined him. For the first time in my life, I heard God's voice, and I had not done anything to 'earn' it. I did not have to read four chapters of Genesis, four chapters of Mark, or three chapters of Psalms to qualify. I did not spend two hours in prayer and fast three days. I was hearing God's voice for the first time simply because my Heavenly Father wanted to talk to me and had things to say. I put down my preconceived perspectives and said yes to an opportunity.

As I pressed in and listened, I began to hear back. I began to hear God, and I could not look back. There was no way I was going back to living life without an intimate relationship with God. As I continued to find myself and God, I took an identity class. That was life-changing for me.

I went on a journey of discovering who I was and who God made me to be. Everything from why I do certain things to why I think the way that I think. I was reaffirming that there was nothing wrong with me and that God created me the exact way I am. It was like ripping the Band-Aid™ off wounds from my past to let them heal. It was a process of stripping away everything that I thought was true in exchange for genuine truth. This was one of the most painful, yet most rewarding processes I have ever been through. It completely changed my life. Now not only could I hear God, but I could begin to live whole, healed, and healthy. Everything I have been through since then has just been such a progression in my relationship with God

Jay joined the prophetic ministry team, and as time went by, I followed him in (much to his surprise). I was just so excited; I dove in headfirst with no hesitations and no regrets. I jumped into the activities like I had been doing them forever, talking to people like I had never spoken to people before and just jumped in with both feet. Jay was shocked that I did not bolt for the door when they had me actively participating, and we laugh about it all the time.

Now I know who God truly is because I hear Him, and He speaks to me. I can hear my Heavenly Father for my kids and other people. I have the deepest desire for everyone to discover how they can hear God and understand Him through authentic relationship. It is not about religion or what I must do to check all the boxes of approval. There is a purpose for why we are created, but sometimes it takes a process of discovery to uncover it.

I do not have a shocking turnaround story. I did not come from the bottom of the barrel and get pulled out and set free. I have always had this desire to be obedient, and now I am good with that. Whatever your story is, never discount it because it is valuable. I now know the difference between being good and being God's. Having a relationship with Him is so different. It is life-changing and creates a space from which I will never go back."

~Connie

We have all been created stunningly unique and have characteristics and talents that shine brighter than the rest. This is called our greatness.

Through purposeful discovery, I learned that creating a list of these attributes helps me to own my significance. I even did this for my son and add new qualities every year on his birthday. With these truths ingrained in his heart and mind, he knows his God-given worth even when his identity is challenged. I start all his statements with the same verbiage, "The greatness I see in you is...."

For me, I have taken this concept a step further. Through prayer, Bible verses, and prophetic words, I have created "I am statements." These declarations solidify who I am as a redeemed daughter of my Heavenly Father. As someone who struggled almost my whole life with depression, this was my salvation in many dark moments. These statements were the lifeline I needed as the enemy attacked my individuality and worth. Like the smooth river stone in David's slingshot, these gems of unwavering, God-breathed truth silenced the taunts of Goliath in my head. It allowed me to own the beautiful, original, exceptional person God created me to be instead of desperately trying to fit in.

(Here are some of my I am statements to inspire you to create your own.)

I am *loved*!
I am a confident daughter and my Abba Father's precious rose.
I am a warrior princess - redeemed and predestined for victory.
I am a fire starter, an igniter of hearts, purpose, and passion.
I am an oak of righteousness planted by the river and bearing much fruit.
I am the bride of Christ – a kept woman!
I am an ambassador – a history maker and world changer.
I am created for extravagance and clothed in creative power.
I am unique – armed with a holy quirkiness.
I am an incredible mother – a bold lioness.
I am an atmosphere changer, empowered with radiant joy and laughter.
I am the sun bearing *the Son*, and this mighty light of mine, I am going to let it shine!

It is said that "I" and "am" are two of the most powerful words you can ever use together because what you put after them creates your reality, and in turn, your destiny. When first stepping into this exercise, it can feel uncomfortable and too good to be true. Remember, view yourself from your Heavenly Father's eyes because He adores who He created you to be.

My Child,

Take a breath and breathe in life. Realize that life is possible because "in the beginning God…" Before anything started or was set in motion, I was there. I am the Author and Creator of all history, all the way down to your specific, detailed story. I am the Composer of the ages, Orchestrator of events that seem to hover in place in perfect timeless suspension. Despite the vast expanse of My loving embrace, I still see you right where you are.

*Think of space and its far-reaching wonder! You can travel for nine years and not reach the end of your galaxy. Yet, My love encompasses every known and unknown corner of **all** the universes. My hand and My heart have touched it all. Think of the intensity and magnitude of that. It is with this virtually limitless love that I love **you**.*

I empathize with every battle you are fighting, the disappointment you are walking through, every break of your heart, and every tear you shed. I see the places you do not feel good enough or worthy, and I am saddened, for I see the untapped greatness I placed in you.

Let Me be your breath when you catch yourself, unable to breathe. Let Me carry you when you cannot find the strength even to stand. Let Me be your hope in the darkness that allows you to endure. Let Me be your stronghold as the walls close in around you and reverse that which the enemy brings down upon you. Let Me be your ability to endure.

Do you know who you are? Do you know how special you are? Do you know how much I love you? Do you realize you are an irreplaceable piece to My mysterious, multifaceted, and miraculous puzzle?

Look at the earth, this amazingly complex world, with all the major components it contains; the sun, the moon, the mountain ranges, volcanoes, valleys, rivers, and oceans; the combination which creates expanses of breathtaking wonder. Do you know that you are also a major component? My favorite component!

You *are more valuable, more special, and more unique than any of those. It is you who I would be the most devastated to lose. I can raise a new mountain from the ground, cause an earthquake to create a river, paint the sky with color every morning and night, allow burning fire to shoot from the core of the earth into the sky, and make melting rock seem to come to life, but there will only ever be one you! I do not clone. I do not try again or redo my children. There will only be one irreplaceable, unchangeable you, with the specific gifts, potential, and authority I placed in you.*

Embrace your life with renewed enthusiasm no matter what your current circumstances. Be moldable, but not breakable. Find your joy, confidence, and be used today, right now, where you are. Let Me take your breath away by the view I will give you as I raise your willing heart to new heights.

*I sent a key to access this full and complete life. The key is My Son, Jesus. He had to pay the ultimate price because I said **you** were worth it, My child. Rejoice, for I brought Him back to life, and because of this, you can live free of sin and condemnation. You have already been forgiven of every sin. All you must do is say, "Yes!" Receive this gift.*

Ready yourself for an adventure because your journey with Me will be far from average. The more willing your heart is, the further I can take you, transform you, and strengthen you.

Renew your hallelujah! Let My Kingdom come through you, my confident child! Let today be the first day of the rest of your life. Let it be Jesus, King of kings and Lord of lords who defines you!

Love you through it all, my majestic masterpiece,
your God, your Heavenly Father, your Creator,
Always and Forever, your Biggest Fan

CHAPTER SIX
"CHURCHY" GIRL

When you write a book with God, guided by the Holy Spirit, you are bound to run into beautiful confirmations that you are doing exactly what you are supposed to be doing. I had no intention of going into so much depth in the last chapter about "I am" statements, but God knew better. The stage is now set to step into this next section with beautiful harmony.

There was a time I walked away from God and religion because I could not see evidence of His tangible presence. I did not want a fake, surface faith, so I decided to prove that God did not exist, or at the very least, prove there was a better substitute for Christianity. Surprisingly, my plan backfired. I concluded that Christianity *was* the best option, but I did not know how to tap into the reality of it. As a direct result of this whole experience, I had a lot of anger towards the church and the labels of religion. This was something that flared its ugly head at a time that I was convinced I had been healed from it.

After many years of being single and walking with God, I had met a guy through online dating that seemed perfect. He said all the right things and painted a picture of genuine interest. I was living redeemed, which allowed me to be bold and honest about my faith and love for God. As it turned out, he found this declaration of faith more interesting than he was interested in me. At one point, it came out that he had dismissed our time together to a friend of his by describing me as "just some churchy girl."

The rage that rose in me because of a simple title shocked me. I had been called much worse in my life, but for some reason, the idea of being attached to such a religious stigma infuriated me. I had a passionate, purposeful relationship with my God that was far outside of the "churchy" box that slammed shut around me as his words hit me full speed. I stewed in my disgust for a while until my Father's voice burst through my rain cloud of contempt. "You are *My* 'churchy' girl, so own it, declare it and claim it as yours!"

"I *am* a "churchy" girl, with its broad, uninspired, and implied definition. This combination of words has somehow decided that my identity is the church. So, mock me with your oversimplified and uneducated words, because as God is my witness, I am: a "Churchy" Girl, a Jesus Freak, a Holy Roller, a Gospel Trumpeter, a Witness, a Radical, a Bible Beater, and Holier than Thou.

My *heart* beats with the rhythm of Heaven because I have found a *hope* that is dependent on a relationship with the Creator of the Universe that I cannot see. My *faith* goes beyond what is tangible and creates a foundation that is unmovable and unshakable. When I *speak,* I speak with life! I speak with joy! I speak with encouragement! I speak with hope! I speak optimism and positivity! I speak until there is a resonating intensity that makes my heart and adrenaline rush!

The shackles and chains that bind you down, that show you your misfortunes, your misses, your insecurities, your faults, and your failures; they are not a permanent place. Rather they are a temporary restraint, grounding you to that which seems impossible to get free of, until you look beyond your own ability and realize you must become more than yourself. You must step out of your own skin and get uncomfortable until you are brought to the place where you do not want to fit the mold anymore. It is in this place that *Jesus* meets you, the real you. He removes the shackles and shows you the image of who He created you to be, and you're free at that moment to step into His freedom and all that He has for you. I proudly claim the title "Jesus Freak" because there is no title in the world that makes sense or could express this *freedom* that I walk in. My Jesus came into the picture, and with just one "YES!", everything changed!

I will witness, holy roll, and trumpet from the top of a mountain the Gospel of my Savior because He is alive! Testimonies of signs, miracles, and wonders do not happen in my life from good teachings; they happen whenever the Creator of the universe is *alive* and well, working *for* me and *through* me. I will wear the stamp of "Bible Beater" because when the world comes against me, the tables turn, and the "crap hits the fan," I know where to turn. I will go to the Bible, Your Word, and I will declare to Heaven for all to hear who the true victory belongs to! I will watch mountains move as I declare the truths that are evident within those pages.

You see empty words written in black on a flimsy page of white, but I see the breath of a living God and see it manifested with a mighty, tangible power. You see scriptures haphazardly thrown out like good luck charms or fortune cookies, but I see nuggets of life-altering realities that can re-chart a course to impossible dreams and raw identity. I stand here vulnerable, yet bold, and I say with absolute conviction that I am "Holier than Thou." Not because I am better than anyone, but because I have gone against myself, and I have let my God win.

I am not perfect, but instead a beautiful work in progress. I gave up who I was pretending to be and gave up the emptiness inside me—clinging to illusions like grains of sand falling through my fingers, making me feel worthy of walking in my own skin. It was in this place that I could be refilled, that I could do the greatest exchange of my life. It was in this place that I went from a slave of the world to Daughter of the Highest King. I am filled with the Holy Spirit, Who directs and guides me daily and equips me with a wisdom that is far beyond the comprehension of my own mind.

Therefore, in the moments when I feel hurt and offended by words haphazardly thrown towards me, I am able, with *supernatural* strength, to channel this hurt into a triumphant anthem that declares who I truly am! Nevertheless, I do not stand apart or in a different category than you. The same God that rescued me, Who has given me strength and propelled me to a place of becoming more than I could possibly imagine, this same God also reaches out to *you*. In a timeless tug-of-war between mind, heart, spirit, and soul, He desires, with everything that is in Him, to welcome you into his loving embrace. I stand here proud to be a "churchy" girl and invite you to join me in a label that will change everything.

Compromising or selling yourself short never gains you anything worth having. For far too many years, I tried to be what everyone else wanted me to be, and it led me to a place of losing myself. I am never alone when I stand with my Heavenly Father in my corner. While the sting of temporary loss may hurt, the confidence of staying true to yourself is priceless. This gave me the momentum to press further into all that God had for me. A fresh fire was kindled to begin to tell my story and the stories of the others whom society would call "eccentrics" and "overzealous."

So, I set pen to paper to heal from the religious stronghold that was suffocating my heart—staring at a blank canvas, hands shaking, and stomach in knots. We, as Christians, are called to "be the church." I broke off the shackles and stepped into full freedom. Like with the "I Am..." statements of character and power, I took back what the enemy was trying to rob me of.

These are the moments that change the course of history. Those are the days that we look back on and remember the instant that changed everything. Whether it be a historical event or in a single individual's momentary blip on the radar, those split-second decisions can allow an atomic bomb of breathtaking faith to be unleashed on the world that will leave it forever transformed.

Will we stay comfortable in our discomfort, or will we step forward into the spotlight that has beckoned us out of the shadows? Do we dare to allow the impossible to flourish in a beautiful array of the unknown? Do we dare to look eccentric?

The God I have become acquainted with does not create us for average, docile, or completely functional lives. He instead implants in us an identity that flexes with each new moment of growth, that expands and contracts with each new breath of belief, and that radiates as the scales fall off our new eyes and we see ourselves through His vision. It is through our quirky uniqueness that His specific fingerprint is allowed to touch this world. As deep calls to deep, we press in, and His response takes us further.

He delights in the way we run through the living garden of His promises. God finds joy as we dance in the rain of shattered glass ceilings, watching them fall like prisms of potential through the sky until they ultimately fuse together, entangled and engulfed in a hope that cannot be shaken.

Notes will be missed as we jump into the quartet that elevates life to a place of serendipitous harmony and creates a concerto of unmeasurable contentment. There is grace in those missed notes, unmatched melodies, and rhythms that do not seem to fit exactly right. My Father calls this jazz!

He keeps the song moving forward, encouraging His son or daughter to hijack the melody and discover what they are truly made of. The spotlight hits you. As the butterflies rise inside of you, the air grows thin, and for an instant, your mind goes blank; it's in these places that bold audacity explodes onto the scene, and fires are ignited that can change the world.

My Father God, the God of Heaven and Earth, the God of stars and seas, the God of all creation, the God of the beginning and all the in-between, the God of the future, and the I Am who will have the final word. *This* God calls you to not simply know of Him, believe in Him, worship Him, or pray to Him, but to *do life* with Him—to experience for the first time in your existence what a true relationship should look like. Far outside of the comprehension of our feeble mind is the offer that slides across the table, signed in blood. The debt is already paid in full. We are free and clear to accept the bonus package that He has negotiated just for us. It is absolutely and completely too good to be true.

He calls us away from coincidences and calls us into a place of seeing the confirmation. He calls us away from relying on luck and calls us to a place of seeing the blessing. He calls us away from working ourselves ragged for any kind of reward and calls us to a place of witnessing doors flying open because of the favor that He desires to bestow upon us. Where will we meet Him? Not in a far off, distant, check in and drop off our list of requests, but rather in a place where we allow ourselves to be seen and, in turn, see Him.

What is it about making that appointment that is so difficult? The answer is different for everyone, but in honestly answering, we discover truths about ourselves that our God has longed to reveal. As we walk away from the long-distance relationship and stop making collect calls to a mysterious Heavenly Father, rather let us make the time for precious visitation in a place where we allow ourselves to be accepted, cherished, and empowered. May the tenacity of His tangible expression of love leave you forever changed and forever hungry for more. You stand before the canvas of possibility. Get outrageous; initiate, and release your exceptional genius on the world. Ready or not, here you come!

I love how beautiful and relatable the Bible is. The life and passion that pours forth continually leaves me in pure wonder. Our Heavenly Father's heart for us comes alive through the pages of this book. As the most read book in the world, there is no doubting that something about this "collection of stories" holds authority and power.

This morning, I sat in my favorite local coffee shop. I became lost in the quiet hum of connection, of joy, and the excitement of caffeine soon hitting the bloodstream, bringing life to the day. A thought slipped into my head as I soaked in the moment. I asked, "God, what do you want to say to me today?" As I opened my laptop and positioned myself to receive the response, I noticed a random tab open on my internet search; with curiosity, I clicked it. I literally laughed out loud because I got totally tickled by my Heavenly Father's goodness and intentionality toward me.

> *"So let's do it—full of belief, confident that we're presentable inside and out. Let's keep a firm grip on the promises that keep us going. He always keeps his word. Let's see how inventive we can be in encouraging love and helping out, not avoiding worshiping together as some do but spurring each other on, especially as we see the big Day approaching."*
>
> *Hebrews 10:23-25 (MSG)*

Do you know what first came to mind as I read this verse? Just do it! Like a delighted Alice in Wonderland, I headed down the rabbit hole of fully discovering what Holy Spirit had given me. I came across this passage from Wikipedia:

> "'Just do it' is a trademark of shoe company Nike™, and one of the core components of Nike's brand. The slogan was coined in 1988 at an advertising agency meeting. The founder of Wieden + Kennedy agency, Dan Wieden, credits the inspiration for his 'Just Do It' Nike™ slogan to Gary Gilmore's last words: 'Let's do it.'"[15] [16]

Now go back and reread the first four words of the verse I had gotten. Confirmation is ignited! Our God, the originator of "Just Do It," speaks through the mysterious

---

[15] (Peters 2021)
[16] (J. W. Peters 2009)

writer of Hebrews. Our Heavenly Father, our Biggest Fan, is cheering us on louder than any other. He knows our strengths and weaknesses more intimately than any other, but still presses us for more and encourages us as we climb.

Although He encourages us with such authority to press into our dreams, He does not expect us to do it alone! He calls to us in the most tangible way, **"Let's** do it." With ultimate conviction, He continues, *"With our power combined, there is no limit to what can be accomplished." What is your impossible dream? Let us step into that and break open your capacity to trust Me"*. God says I am capable!

We have a choice to make every day when we wake up— a choice to stay the same or make one small step towards a new level of who we were designed to be. If God is not worried, then why do I worry? Simple. It is because of my lack of trust in the true authority of my Creator. I must continually start over, not because I have failed, but because I give up too soon when self-doubt creeps in. This book is the perfect example. I received a word from the Lord telling me to write, with confirmation and specific instructions laid out like blinking arrows in the dark. Regrettably, I did not press into this assignment with the eagerness that I should have at first.

You can possibly relate to the deafening berating of excuses that came rushing in. "I do not have a formal 'higher' education; I have never written anything of substance. I do not have a platform or following. Have I mentioned I do not know how to write?" Oh, the lies we try and tell ourselves to keep us from going to the next level—carefully twisted half-truths that the enemy plants in our minds to keep us wading in the mediocrity of life. God's truth opens the door to opportunity.

I do not have a formal "higher" education, but I have been to the school of the Holy Spirit and have been taken to high places with my God. Through this, I have gained understanding, motivating me to dig into the truths of my Lord of Heaven and Earth. He has brought me to places of revelation on matters of the body, spirit, and soul. Holy Spirit was given to us to fill in the gaps that we need in any given moment; we only need to believe and step in.

I have never written anything of substance, but when God opens a door of opportunity for us, He never asks us for our resume of past accomplishments. He is simply not interested in our qualifications but rather what our total abandonment in Him can generate. Honestly, the more unqualified we are to accomplish something, the greater the glory God gets out of it. As I sat with the keyboard before me, beautiful, life-giving words began to flow that astonished me. Connections were made to what I thought were random prophetic scribblings, and they were infused into the manuscript. Holy magic was happening, and I was ecstatic. Furthermore, I was reminded that if God orchestrates something, He will be your greatest promoter.

I do not have a platform or following, but my God has placed many amazing influential people in my life who have powerful voices with multitudes who listen. I believe that you are reading this right now because God created this as an appointment between you and Him. I am simply the "churchy" girl who said, "Yes," and allowed God's voice to flow through me to you. What is God asking you to step into that you have been putting off or making excuses about? I challenge you to fully embrace your identity in Him and "Just do it!"

May the tenacity of His tangible expression of love leave you forever changed and forever hungry for more. You stand before the canvas of possibility. Get outrageous; initiate, and release your exceptional genius on the world. Ready or not, here you come!

CHAPTER SEVEN
VIBRATIONS OF HEAVEN

Christianity often gets lumped into the broad category of monotone religion. In turn, most skeptics separate a belief in God from their concept of reality. At one point in my life, I drew this very distinct and bold line between what made sense to me, that which was able to be experienced, tested, measured, and/or observed, and everything else, which included my faith in God. This created what I thought was a very safe place in which every variable could be controlled. The actuality of this was that I was simply boxing myself in, in a way that kept me blinded from the existence of what I already knew to be true. When I got to a place where I decided to break the suffocating walls down, I came face-to-face with the reality that I had created for myself and the opposing force of the reality I wanted to experience.

So, what really is reality? According to Wikipedia,[17]
1) reality is the state of things as they exist, rather than as they may appear or might be imagined.[18]
2)Reality includes everything that is and has been, whether it is observable or comprehensible[19] and,
3) a still broader definition includes "that which has existed, exists, or will exist."[20]

I was remarkably familiar with the first definition, but the second and third definitions threw me for a loop and

---

[17] (Wikipedia n.d.)
[18] (Oxford Lexico n.d.)
[19] (Collins 2018)
[20] (Descartes, Haldane and Ross 1911)

caused me to pursue a journey that left me forever changed. The fact of the matter was that I was looking for a God to fit inside *my* comprehension, to be able to be explained within the simplicity of *my* mind and *my* understanding. The Heavenly Father that I found is far beyond comprehension.

His wisdom, love, knowledge, mercy, faithfulness, strength, understanding, and grace is far beyond anything I could fathom. Suppose I am seeking something more than my limited perspective and understanding. I need a God that is far bigger than anything in my sphere of conception. I desire to seek the answers and direction for my life from the One who breathed life into humanity and fashioned all creation with a word. *Faith*, at its very root, is a reality that includes far more than what is observable or comprehensible outside of belief.[21] I did not understand this concept until I stepped fully into what God had for me. As I trusted before I understood, a reaction took place that accelerated me into a deeper understanding of the Kingdom of God. Consequently, my reality has become an irreversible faith.

My passionate pursuit of Christ and my Heavenly Father led me directly to Holy Spirit. I will be honest; I did not know Holy Spirit outside of seeming like a third wheel and possibly a ghost-like "thing." (Raised in a Lutheran church, we never talked about the subject, which left me unable to associate and question if I should.) I had no radar for the supernatural and did not believe that miracles, signs, and wonders were something applicable for today. It was powerful to read about in the Bible, but at that time, my understanding of the book of Acts was kind of like a far-fetched sci-fi novel; it was fascinating, but impossible.

---

[21] (Bunnin and Tsui-James 2008)

If you are like I was and have no radar for the Holy Spirit, let me introduce you to the tangible, relational, very important third part of the Holy Trinity. Based on the research of Dr. Jim Denison, the CEO of Denison Forum and expressed in his article, '*Who is Holy Spirit?*'[22] the Spirit is a Person who operates directly and individually. He is not an "it," more than a "presence," and not a "phantom," nor a "ghost." There are many more examples, but the fact of the matter is the Holy Spirit is God, and consequently, He matters a great deal.

Jesus taught us to pray in Matthew,[23] *"Your kingdom come, your will be done, on earth as it is in heaven."* In that verse, He revealed the need for a transfer of glory. Holy Spirit is that conduit of the Kingdom. We get the awesome privilege of partnering with God to bring His wisdom to Earth and infiltrate the systems that need resurrection and restructuring.

We have access to this wisdom via Holy Spirit, who came on the scene after Jesus laid out the groundwork of understanding for who He is. As detailed in John 14, Jesus explains,

> *"If you love me, keep my commands. And I will ask the Father, and he will give you another advocate to help you and be with you forever— the Spirit of truth. The world cannot accept him because it neither sees him nor knows him. But you know him, for he lives with you and will be in you. All this I have spoken while still with you. But the Advocate, the Holy Spirit, whom the Father will send in my name, will teach you*

---

[22] (Denison 2019)
[23] (BibleGateway n.d.)

all things and will remind you of everything I have said to you. Peace I leave with you; my peace I give you. I do not give to you as the world gives. Do not let your hearts be troubled and do not be afraid."[24]

Everything in all of God-breathed creation operates in harmony—from the ebb and flow of the ocean tides to the transition of seasons with perfect synchronization. As such, there must be harmony within the Godhead. The thoughts of all three are in complete unison, forming and constructing all things. In 1 Corinthians 2:10-11 (NIV), the word states,

"these are the things God has revealed to us by his Spirit. The Spirit searches all things, even the deep things of God. For who knows a person's thoughts except their own spirit within them? In the same way no one knows the thoughts of God except the Spirit of God."

With the Spirit knowing the thoughts of God, He can transfer that wisdom, as was evident in Jesus' life—teaching Him, being the source of His wisdom, and working miracles through the Spirit.

Jesus, our Messiah, was the first example in humanity of what was truly possible when we are filled with the power and authority of Heaven. The Holy Spirit still speaks today, which is especially evident as we read the scriptures. Scriptures are words coming alive as the Spirit reveals the life that is established within the ink and paper. The mystical things of God are revealed and understood through this

---

[24] (BibleGateway n.d.)

supernatural wisdom. While He is still active in every believer's life, the extent is completely reliant on the individual. Our free will is never tampered with, so it is vital that we choose to pursue Holy Spirit with a very real relationship.

Stepping past who Holy Spirit *is*, we ask the question, "What does He *do*?" This can more easily be understood by looking at *what* He did. He did not just arrive on the scene to shake things up, but has always been present and active from the beginning of time. Genesis 1:2 says that the, "...the *Spirit of God was hovering...*", ready, active, and empowered to bring transformation to the lifeless and void. He continued to do this through the ministry, life, and resurrection of Jesus. Jesus was born of the Spirit and worked miracles, bringing life and hope through the power of the Spirit.

We have been given access to the Holy Spirit, the same Spirit that raised Jesus from the dead; we simply must ask. As we invite Him into our heart, mind, and spirit, a shift will take place, aligning us with the intention of the Kingdom. Holy Spirit may force us to confront and acknowledge our sin, but He will never condemn us or disqualify us from grace. Condemnation from the enemy drives us to despair and hopelessness. Conviction, in contrast, forces us to face the truth and gives us the opportunity to repent and change. Holy Spirit is also our comforter, joy, and hope.

The Spirit is *Holy* and is the tangible expression of the Father and Son to allow us to operate at our fullest capacity of the greatness we were designed to be. Being created to be known and to know our Heavenly Father happens through the transaction of the Holy Spirit. The most tangible, yet unknown, member of the Trinity.

There are so many powerful, beautiful verses that further give characterization to Holy Spirit. Such as:

"He reveals deep and hidden things; he knows what lies in darkness, and light dwells with him."

Daniel 2:22 (NIV)

"Arise, shine; For your light has come! And the glory of the Lord is risen upon you. For behold, the darkness shall cover the earth, and deep darkness the people; But the Lord will arise over you, And His glory will be seen upon you."

Isaiah 60:1-2 (NKJV)

"For the Spirit God gave us does not make us timid, but gives us power, love, and self-discipline."

2 Timothy 1:7 (NIV)

"You were taught, with regard to your former way of life, to put off your old self, which is being corrupted by its deceitful desires; to be made new in the attitude of your minds; and to put on the new self, created to be like God in true righteousness and holiness. Therefore, each of you must put off falsehood and speak truthfully to your neighbor, for we are all members of one body. 'In your anger do not sin': Do not let the sun go down while you are still angry, and do not give the devil a foothold. Anyone who has been stealing must steal no longer, but must work, doing something useful with their own hands, that they may have

something to share with those in need. Do not let any unwholesome talk come out of your mouths, but only what is helpful for building others up according to their needs, that it may benefit those who listen. And do not grieve the Holy Spirit of God, with whom you were sealed for the day of redemption. Get rid of all bitterness, rage, and anger, brawling and slander, along with every form of malice. Be kind and compassionate to one another, forgiving each other, just as in Christ God forgave you."

Ephesians 4:22-32 (NIV)

"Make every effort to keep the unity of the Spirit through the bond of peace. There is one body and one Spirit, just as you were called to one hope when you were called; one Lord, one faith, one baptism, one God and Father of all, who is over all and through all and in all."

Ephesians 4: 3-6 (NIV)

With distinctly different personality traits, Father, Son, and Holy Spirit function with minds that are perfectly in sync—always with the same intent, passion, love, and commitment to us. That is hard to fathom. They literally never disagree about anything because they operate as one, within pure truth and clear vision. When we ask, Holy Spirit resides within us, giving us His same clarity, truth, and vision if we tap into it. Like plugging into the power cord of the Kingdom, we have the ability through our cohesion with Christ to know the thoughts of God because He gave us His mind.

The vibration of Heaven becomes our cadence as we bring Heaven down to tangible Earth. The "spiritual gifts" He bestows upon us at our salvation can have a powerful impact. These are simply ways in which we can know and serve God more efficiently. Staying true to the unique design God put in each of us, our gifts differ from each other. Examples found from various lists in the Bible are: administration, apostleship, discernment, evangelism, exhortation, faith, giving, healing, intercession, interpretation of tongues, knowledge, leadership, mercy, miracles, prophecy, serving, shepherding, speaking in tongues, teaching, and wisdom. These can be revealed to us directly, as Holy Spirit speaks to us. Godly believers can help with direction and revelation. Giving attention to your opportunities for service, combined with your interests, passions, and abilities can give insight into your gifts. If you wish to dig deeper into your "spiritual DNA," there are many spiritual gift analysis tools available today. When you find and use your spiritual gifts, you will find the passion, purpose, and peace of God.

More evidence of Holy Spirit's presence and authenticity in scripture, which can also be experienced today, are found in Acts 2:1-3 (NIV).

"When the day of Pentecost came; they were all together in one place. Suddenly a sound like the blowing of a violent wind came from heaven and filled the whole house where they were sitting. They saw what seemed to be tongues of fire that separated and came to rest on each of them. All of them were filled with the Holy Spirit and began to speak in other tongues as the Spirit enabled them."

The understanding of this verse is that when the Spirit came at Pentecost, each Christian began speaking in a "heavenly prayer language," an "unknown tongue." Being able to communicate in this way allows sons and daughters of God to speak to their Father in a language known only to the individual's spirit. When this gift is used within scriptural guidelines, it draws those who practice it closer to the Father.

By being submitted to the leading of God's Spirit each day, our spiritual gifts will fulfill His purpose, to His glory, and our good. Being able to operate in a prayer language does not make anyone "more spiritual," and there is nothing wrong with you if it is not something you desire. (I am adding this detailed explanation because this is what I wanted to know was possible when I was beginning my passionate journey of faith.)

I was not satisfied with stagnant religion, but wanted to experience the fullness of joy that we were promised in the Word. I wanted to step past my doubts, preconceived notions, and fear of the unknown. It is amazing how when we step away from our understanding, God meets us and opens the door to experiencing our predetermined "impossible." I was able to discover this firsthand as I walked out the beginning of my Holy Spirit adventure.

Now, I am quite stubborn in nature, but my God created me perfectly and has taught me to redeem all the qualities that make me, me. Without that stubbornness, I would not have such a testimony of discovery to write about. God uses all things for His good.

One day at the end of a church service about Holy Spirit, the pastor said that if anybody wanted to be baptized in the Holy Spirit, they should come forward. I was stubborn and skeptical, but I wanted everything that God had for me, so I decided to go down and get prayed for, just to see if it was real.

I thought that people who prayed in tongues or fell to the ground were crazy people and were most definitely pretending for attention. Despite this, I was willing to give it a try. My heart was fluttering with each step, half-hoping that it would be real. I begged God to give it to me, too, and half-tried to prepare myself for disappointment.

A beautiful, sweet-spirited woman prayed for me, and I felt my adrenaline begin to rush. She prayed a beautiful prayer that I truly remember little of, but the heavens didn't rumble, lightning didn't crack through the ceiling, and I didn't suddenly lose all control of my mind and body. At the end, she whispered, "I can see in the Spirit that you can pray in tongues if you simply open your mouth and believe."

I was instantly thrilled and petrified. I did not want to do it wrong, and performance anxiety took over. I smiled sweetly back, nodded, and walked away. Much to my surprise, where I thought disappointment would surely be, was anticipation and excitement. I could not let this moment pass. As the church was busily letting out and the next service was filling the walkways and halls, I slipped into a nearby bathroom and hid in a stall. Sitting on a toilet, I sent the tiniest of prayers up, "Yes Lord, Yes!" I opened my mouth, and somehow, I knew what to do.

It did not start with a Sunday sermon preached powerfully in a foreign language that I supernaturally knew (but that is not impossible), it started as clicking noises and sounds, but I knew this was *my* prayer language! It may have seemed so insignificant to another, but those clicks were mine and filled me with the Holy Spirit so intensely I almost fell off the toilet seat as I cried for joy and thanked God over and over.

I learned as I chased after my new gift, that like any other ability, praying in tongues must be practiced to be enhanced. The more you work this muscle and press into Holy Spirit, the more your faith will grow, and your language will enhance.

Today, I speak fluently in a language I do not know to my God in Heaven, and it activates His will, heart, and intention for every situation. When I do not know what to pray or simply have no words, I pray in tongues and connect Heaven to Earth. It expands my capacity and links up with the governing hierarchy of Heaven in a tangible way.

The same way we accept Christ as our Lord and Savior and have faith that we are saved, so we can receive Holy Spirit. Jesus simplified it so beautifully in Luke 11:13 (NKJV), *"If you then, being evil, know how to give good gifts to your children, how much more will your heavenly Father give the Holy Spirit to those who ask Him!"* That not so little "yes" brought a new level of JOY that transformed everything.

JOY
JUST.
ONE.
YES.

"Just One Yes" allows the Father to come in and radically transform your life. "Just One Yes" brings hope and promise. "Just One Yes" takes our nothing and makes something radical. "Just One Yes" calls dry bones back to life. "Just One Yes" creates a spontaneous metamorphosis that becomes both sustainable and irreversible! With "Just One

Yes," you realize you are *loved*. With "Just One Yes," you can tap into *greatness*! With "Just One Yes," you can walk into your *identity*! With "Just One Yes," you can have *hope*! With "Just One Yes," you will **never** be the same! YES, LORD, YES!

***

Holy Spirit is with us and in us to help perfect our faith by being beacons of change and hope to those we encounter. In this experience, 1 Corinthian 2: 9-11 became very real, as Danyal discovered just how true our God in Heaven is.

> *"However, as it is written: 'What no eye has seen, what no ear has heard, and what no human mind has conceived'—the things God has prepared for those who love him—these are the things God has revealed to us by his Spirit. The Spirit searches all things, even the deep things of God. For who knows a person's thoughts except their own spirit within them? In the same way no one knows the thoughts of God except the Spirit of God."*

Danyal's yes, as she will explain, took her to levels with God she never thought possible.

> *"I've been a Christian all my life, and there have been times where I have gone to church and not gone to church, but I always knew that there was a God. Despite this, I always still had the questions, "Is He real? Does He really know how many hairs on your head?"*

My husband and I had just started seeking the Lord. We sought after Holy Spirit with hope and anticipation. Researching and taking classes on the Holy Spirit was not enough. There was a conference in town where a man named Tony Kemp was going to speak. He gave a wonderful sermon, and then he started healing people. I thought that was awesome and wanted to have that ability. Later in the conference, he called me to the front. He gave me a prophetic word where he told me, 'I know exactly what's been going on in your life for the past five years; the devil has been attacking you. Once he lets you rest, he attacks you again. You will rest, but he's been constantly attacking your family.' He told me exactly how he attacked us every single time. Tony declared, 'We're breaking that off you now. We are releasing you from the enemy. He is not going to attack you again. God's going to give you financial freedom. He's going to give you a promotion in your job, and God is going to bring a connection to you.'

At that moment, I knew for sure that my Heavenly Father really knew how many hairs I had on my head because He knew exactly what I had been through. I felt completely loved and that I was going to be okay. One year later, I had a promotion in my job, I had paid off a lot of financial debt, and today, I am partnering with God to help people. Experiencing the gifts that He bestows on you is such an amazing experience."

~Danyl

"The same way we accept Christ as our Lord and Savior and have faith that we are saved, so we can receive Holy Spirit."

CHAPTER EIGHT
PEACE

"I have told you these things, so that in me you may have peace. In this world you will have trouble. But take heart! I have overcome the world."

John 16:33 (NIV)

Peace in the world is the absence of something, such as noise, fear, or distractions. Peace in the Kingdom is the presence of something, such as hope, spirit, faith, or victory. The definition of peace is freedom from disturbance, also described as tranquility or a state or period when there is no war, or the war is ended.[25] So, peace, in its very nature, is contradictory to most people's "normal."

Life today is often lived in a continuous state of anxiety and confrontation. This is not what our good Father intended for us. Jesus even said in John 14: 27 (NIV), *"Peace I leave with you; my peace I give you. I do not give to you as the world gives. Do not let your hearts be troubled and do not be afraid."* I am convinced that if Jesus left something for us, He probably thought it important to have and knew we would have a deficiency in it, so if this is something we have, why is it so hard to access? I believe the parable of how Jesus calms the storm gives us some answers to this very question.

"That day when evening came, he said to his disciples, 'Let us go over to the other side.'

---

[25] (Oxford Lexico n.d.)

Leaving the crowd behind, they took him along, just as he was, in the boat. There were also other boats with him. A furious squall came up, and the waves broke over the boat, so that it was nearly swamped. Jesus was in the stern, sleeping on a cushion. The disciples woke him and said to him, 'Teacher, don't you care if we drown?' He got up, rebuked the wind and said to the waves, 'Quiet! Be still!' Then the wind died down and it was completely calm. He said to his disciples, 'Why are you so afraid? Do you still have no faith?' They were terrified and asked each other, 'Who is this? Even the wind and the waves obey him!'"

Mark 4: 35-41 (NIV)

I have read and studied this scripture countless times. It truly is one of my favorites because it shows us the raw, human side of the disciples. This gives me hope for my own walk with Christ. Coming across this scripture, again, revealed a new truth I felt compelled to share! It was that last verse that I kept reading over and over; verse 41, *"They were terrified and asked each other, 'Who is this? Even the wind and the waves obey him!'"* The word that jumped off the page and hit me like a thousand bricks; **terrified**. Trusted friends, confidantes, witnesses to countless miracles became **terrified** of Jesus. Why? Two truths came to light as I asked Father, "what caused the fear?"

First was the fact that at this moment, the disciples came face to face with the "bigness" of God. They saw the breathtaking wonder of who the I Am is and the power He has, even over the wind and the waves. They could wrap their minds around the relationship, the miracles, and the signs of

Christ, but in this instant, God flew out of the box of human understanding and comprehension in a wondrous display. We read this often and think, "Why would they be scared? They know Jesus, that's crazy." I thought this for a while, too, but God spoke to me and revealed something incredible and humbling. Is our faith so *comfortable* that we have lost the *fear* of God? Are we taking authority over the storms in our lives? Is anxiety and depression creeping in from our lack of faith to speak to those storms? As we pray, are we looking for an elaborate, perfect solution, remedy, or plan to set in motion, or are we scared the solution is so simple, and we somehow keep missing it?

I think part of the fear that the disciples experienced came from the simplicity of the command. With *faith*, we command peace, and it shall be so! Done. So, what are you over-complicating? Step up, son, and stand up, daughter of the Almighty God; *command* that storm to stop, and have the faith to experience His perfect peace!

Another truth that was revealed so beautifully to me was, when we walk in the ultimate peace of our Heavenly Father, *not everyone is going to understand.* There is going to be a disconnect as people look upon what they do not understand. It might manifest in different ways, but the root is the same. If the loving friends of Jesus could become terrified of their teacher as He walked in His identity, how much more will the world look with confusion upon sons and daughters of the Kingdom? Is the fear of what people will think holding you back from fully embracing the power and authority that Christ went to the cross to give you?

It is in this place of fear that love and grace come in! We cannot push away those who have little faith, because most likely, we were also there at some point. Furthermore, by getting angry with their lack of peace, faith, hope, or love, we can create our own personal storm.

We need to love people, friends, and family wherever they are in their journey, and give them grace and hope to be able to find the peace that you have. *Be* their hope. Stand in the gap for them and command peace to their storm. Set the example of Christ that cannot help but point to the extraordinary nature of our God!

Despite the disciples' obvious bewilderment from the recent events, they continued across the lake. I am guessing it was probably a noticeably quiet boat ride as everyone processed the experience. What stands out to me is that as Jesus gets out of the boat, He is instantly met by what would seem to be a much larger problem. A mad man possessed by "a legion of demons"[26] bombards Him. Jesus handles the situation, casts the demons out of the man and into thousands of pigs, and they drown themselves in the water. During this entire encounter, it is not recorded that the disciples said anything. They were literally just full of fear of a storm, but in the face of a "legion of demons," they have nothing to say?

I heard a pastor preach about how, on the boat, after processing through their fear, they received Jesus' peace. They were able to rest in the confidence of Him Who called them because of the power residing *inside* them. There are several more accounts of Jesus having to continue to remind the disciples not to fear or have courage. At that moment, though, they were able to walk in the victory of the Almighty and experience the power of God's peace.

---

[26] (BibleGateway n.d.)

***

To be able to walk in peace, you must have the revelation of God's goodness and intentional love for you. Without this foundation, the storms of life will continue to tear you down and keep you in the rip current of repetitive behavior. This truth is powerfully evident in the next testimony of one of the strongest women I know, Shellie.

"My story of when I knew God was for me, speaking to me and loving me, took place at a Christian weekend retreat. It was called Walk to Emmaus, and I was participating in October of 2008. I was not sure what to expect during this weekend, but I knew that I wanted more in my life.

I had a very, very toxic and dysfunctional childhood. It was filled with neglect, poverty, sexual and emotional abuse, including witnessing my brothers being physically abused by my father. As a byproduct of this, in my mind, God was very distant and very harsh. I was looking through those lenses and comparing my Heavenly Father with my earthly father. I had gone to church with my grandmother, off and on between elementary and middle school, and then a little bit in high school. It was really to escape my father's house.

At the time of this retreat, I had been married for eight years. It was also very dysfunctional and toxic. My husband had many of the same characteristics as my father. Grasping a bit of desperation, I had no idea what to expect. I had several walls of reservation and unbelief at the beginning of the weekend, but my change came the third night, after a very intimate worship experience called 'Candlelight.' (It is incredibly special! I feel like it represents a glimpse into heaven.) After candlelight, we were invited to stay in the chapel where service took place, and pray, talk or just be alone with our thoughts and God. My prayers were, up until that point, basic and boring. I kind of fell asleep at night praying. I would lay down, start my prayer, not sure how to pray, and certainly not knowing that I had been hearing God all along, I would eventually drift off to sleep. I did not really know how to pray.

I remember noticing the chapel's beautiful stained-glass windows. They captivated me with their beauty. I did not want to stop feeling the way I was feeling in this beautiful moment. I felt good. I could tangibly feel the love in the room. So, I stayed. I sat at the back of the chapel praying. I was thinking, just how beautiful the candlelight was and how I felt loved. I even asked myself questions like, 'What is this feeling? How is this happening? Is this real?' Then a thought dropped in my mind. I heard the Lord say, 'Go to the front of the chapel by the podium and speak to the pastor that was up there.' He was just waiting, reading his Bible, and hanging out to see if anyone needed prayer or wanted to talk.

I responded with a very definite, 'Oh, no, I'm not going up to the front.' Then I hear it again, 'Go up to the front and talk to the guy.' I was arguing in my mind and creating excuses and disqualifying myself with things like, 'What am I supposed to say when I get up there? I am going to sound like an idiot. I'll just be standing there, awkwardly not saying anything.' I continued this for a while and then finally thought, 'Maybe this is God talking to me.' I said, 'All right, God, if this is really You, please just send him to come stand beside me because I really don't want to move or go up there and sound like an idiot. Then, the next time I hear You, if this is You, I'll do what you say.'

At that moment I looked up, and he was standing right beside me. I started laughing at first from the reality and shock that this was real. This is real! God loves me. He is talking to me; He sees me and is willing to respond. Oh, my goodness, I matter to Him! That was wild to me. At this time, I had not really mattered to anyone on the earth. (I mean, that I could tell.) No one ever acted like they loved me. My father and mother surely did not. My grandmother did, but she was hardcore Church of Christ; therefore, she did not let those feelings show. Consequently, at that time, I really did not know how much she loved me. So, this Pastor named Royce was standing next to me and said, 'Shellie, God told me to come and stand beside you, and He has a word for you. He wants me to tell you that He loves you and He sees you. He knows that you have been through some hard things, but He is right there with you. He is so proud of you.'

These words changed my world. It rocked me! The unconditional love that I felt just to be seen by Him and to know that He is nothing like my earthly father. I still struggled with this for several years after that, but at that moment, I knew He was different. I came to understand just how different, as He has continued to reveal Himself to me. I love the person I'm becoming because I know God and how much He loves me."

~Shellie

When someone encounters the love of God, it brings peace to the storms of life and purpose to the rain. This peace is transformational as a life done with Jesus is cultivated. We will never know (on this side of Heaven) why bad things happen. This is a question I struggled with for a long time. What I do know is that from these incidences, seeds become planted in the darkness. God can create good from all things, including these great tragedies. The longer it takes for the seed to burst through the surface, the more deeply the roots have begun to infuse with His renewing strength.

I am here to tell you whether you are reading this from a jail cell or the comfort of your favorite chair, our Heavenly Father cares about every one of us—even those pieces that you do not tell people about. May you find healing, love, and peace as you feel Holy Spirit meet you right where you are.

CHAPTER NINE
BEAUTIFULLY UNBALANCED

At one point in the writing of this book, my prophetic pastor approached me about sharing my testimony. My initial reaction was, "No way!" You see, several months leading up to that appointment, God was taking me through a season of emptying me of everything that I thought was a solid foundation. This forced me into a place of vulnerability and brutal honesty. I was still in a place of unbalance, so I did not think I had anything to testify to.

One of Satan's favorite lies is that we must have it all together before God can use us. The irony is almost humorous. Here, God called me to write this book, and with zero idea on how to execute such a task, I jumped right in. When asked for my testimony, I wanted to run and hide. Thank goodness for God's abundant grace.

As I sat down to write, I thought I would make it easy and testify to what God has already done. This is the highlight reel of my life. You do not become a survivor through an easy life, but by walking through hell and coming out the other side with the promise of restoration. Everyone's journey looks different, so never diminish what you have been through or what has wounded you compared to someone else. Likewise, if your story is ten more shades of dark and terrifying, do not think that God cannot reach you. Light never has to fight darkness, because when light enters, the darkness is instantly pushed back.

I supposed I could testify to how God restored the fire of a fourteen-year-old girl, fourteen years later. This girl grew up in the church and wanted all of Jesus, but the world slammed a basket of disapproval over her fire and snuffed it out. It seemed being obsessed with her Heavenly Father a bad thing, so she cowered back into her unseen corner. God created her to be all *in*, but since that was not acceptable, she made an inner vow to be all *out*. Jesus overcame, and He sweetly won back her heart and launched her into a destiny of purpose with Him at the center.

I could testify to the power of forgiveness. Like I touched on earlier, I came out of an unhealthy six-year relationship bruised and broken. Not only facing the reality that I still had to share custody of my precious son with this "monster," but I was trapped in a part of the country where I literally had no one because this man decided he wanted to be a father. Nonetheless, God healed me. He loved me to a place of forgiving him and promised to protect me as He forced me to invite him to church. I watched the "monster" I had been terrified of for years accept Christ, get baptized, and transform into a man of honor. We won't get back together, but my son has been blessed by this shift.

I could testify to truly accepting forgiveness and hearing God's voice for myself as I sought to heal from an abortion that took place at one of my lowest points. Or I could testify to how God rescued me from drugs, alcohol, and a terrifying lifestyle and set me on a new path of all-in to follow Him.

Alas, none of these were right. Nothing takes us down like the hit we do not see coming, which is what happened to me. In an instant, with no warning, no explanation, and no real reason, my joy vanished. The joy that was the very center of my recrafted identity came crashing down, and I felt lost and empty. Like Thor without his hammer, my not-so-secret weapon was taken from me.

At first, I got angry. I pursued and cursed the enemy and every demon I thought could be responsible. I came to understand, through pressing in with raw desperation, that my Heavenly Father was taking me to a place of vulnerability and unbalance so that I could truly reach new levels with Him. The process of reaching these new levels, however? They suck.

It would be great if when God calls us to a new spiritual level, to take on the next mountain standing in our way, that we could go on a seven day, all-expense paid, spiritual cruise where we handle the issue and come back refreshed. But that's not how life works. During the "suck," life still must go on, and we can choose to hide or to press forward. While pressing on, we rely upon the life-giving manna of our Father to supply what we need every day when we are lacking.

There was a time in my walk when I thought, "I should have it all together," but my Father was taking me to a new place of clearing the slate. I had to be weak when I wanted to be strong, I had to be unsure in a place I wanted to have confidence, and I had to be led through the unknown valley when I was comfortable being a leader. I got so hurt and resentful several times. Even as I received prophetic words that spoke to me being "so full of joy" and "igniting atmospheres with my joy," I was barely keeping a smile on my face and screamed internally.

"Father," I prayed, "why don't they see me? Why can't they see what's happening to me and that I'm lacking?"

"My daughter," He responded, *"because you have asked, you have received. I am your supply while under construction, so you lack nothing!"*

*(I tell you about what I have been through beforehand in order to give you an understanding. Despite everything that I've walked out of, **this** was the most painful thing I had ever been through.)*

At one point, depression and loneliness, compiled with prayers left unanswered, promises unfulfilled, and a feeling of being stuck in every aspect of my life, came crashing in. I felt like I was actually suffocating and stuck, not in a valley, but a hole. Everything I did was just making the hole deeper, so I mustered all my religious dialect and literally screamed at God, "What the hell!?" He was faithful and met me during worship, at what I knew was a God appointment, and spoke to me so very sweetly.

Before *I share the word/vision that He gave me, you have to understand a bit of backstory.*

My son was diagnosed with severe ADHD, but before we knew what was happening, he would get himself so worked up at times, he would have violent outbursts caused by him feeling out of control and scared. The only thing that would help was when I would grab him in my arms. Even as he kicked and screamed violently, I would continue to hold him against me as tight as possible—not speaking, just holding. He would thrash and try to wriggle out of my grasp, but I would continue to hold him tightly. Eventually, he would run out of strength, go limp, and start crying because he was so scared. Once the crying would stop, he would hug me as I exaggerated my breaths so that he would mimic me and begin to breathe deeply. It was here, and only here at this moment that he could hear me or comprehend what I was saying. At that place, at that moment, I would begin to speak to him, soothe him, tell him it would be okay and how special he was.

Back to the vision God showed me. This was what our Heavenly Father spoke to me, *"This has been you, My love. You are fighting against yourself for reasons you are not even fully aware of. You're angry because you have not seen the manifestation of years of heard prayers. You are scared to pursue promises for fear of disappointment. That hole you feel suffocated by is not a hole; it is my embrace, loved one. I am holding you tight, squeezing the life out of you because I have **My** life to give you. Listen to the rhythm of My breathing as I breathe into your lungs the oxygen necessary to go to new atmospheres where you have been called, and I have made a way. Quiet your body and your mind and give up. I am ready and eager to speak, but I need you to be in the mindset to listen and fully grasp everything I have for you. You will receive back your joy, but your secret weapon will shift to authenticity through radical faith."*

This shifted something in me that has truly been a game-changer. I can declare that every rough patch I have gone through, "I am *glad* it happened!" Before I even see the fruit of why I had to go through it, with each trial preparing me for triumph, I have big prayers, bigger promises, and a radical destiny. Even though I have not seen it fulfilled yet, I declare I will! There is a process, a beautiful unbalancing when unlocking the destiny which God has for me. While going through this, I did not need a quick fix. or a coffee cup verse; I simply needed reassurance that I would make it and God was with me.

Without those testimonies and trials of the past, without the places that I had to recalculate and figure out how to find the strength to get through, I wouldn't have the fire burning inside of me to blast me to the new levels that would take me to new atmospheres to seek His Holy face. Time after time, it is in those places of course-correcting that we can go from *knowing* to *experiencing* the wonder that there is no place sweeter than His embrace and that Christ alone is the reason why.

(I feel He had me share this because others are in the middle of their own processes, feeling unbalanced and needing to know they are not alone. So, whoever you are, Father is there with you, and you will make it. It may be the hits we do not see coming that take us down the hardest, but all of Heaven is cheering for us to get back up! I got knocked down, but I did not get knocked out, and I pray the same for you!)

***

This place of experiencing being unbalanced took Danielle from wavering to creating a foundation of unwavering faith.

"I was raised in the church, and I learned early on that just because you go to a building does not mean you have a relationship with God. I got to a point where I decided I wanted to control my own life. I was following rules put in place by an entity I had never met, and that no longer sat

well with me. The results were not the best and created an unhealthy unbalance in my life.

Eventually, I came back to church, but it was by force. I was told I could not live where I was if I was not in church. I had to change my ways and shift the direction my life was heading. This turned into a Godsend situation.

I started going back to church with my aunt and uncle. They hung out with these crazy people at church who loved Holy Spirit and Jesus so much. They just loved being in His presence and experiencing more of what He had to offer. This was such a foreign concept to me at this time in my life. Slowly but surely, as we went, I let go of all my resentment. The Lord thawed my heart and showed me that these people were not crazy. He continued to express, 'These people aren't weird; this is what I have for My people. This is what I've made My children to do.'

Fast forward to another time, when a couple came as guest speakers to the prophetic church class I had been attending. As we worshiped, Holy Spirit came in such a tangible way that I was slain in the Spirit for the first time. (Being slain in the Spirit just simply means that you become so overwhelmed with the presence and love of God that nothing else matters, and present reality often fades away. This can be experienced as falling, shaking, lying on the ground, or dancing.)

I do not know how long I was affected. I could not eat or drink. I could not do anything because I just had so much of the Father's love. He really is who He says He is, and what He is was just so powerful. I felt that powerful love wrapped around me. I could not even move. After that, I finally *realized I wanted to get serious about this because God **is** real. He cares about me to the extent that He can take away everything that I have done with His grace and replace it with a crazy love that I have never felt before. Even growing up in the church and being religious could not hint at the authenticity that was possible with my Heavenly Father. You've never experienced love until you find it for yourself, and it will change everything.*

For me, it took becoming so overwhelmed that I could not even eat. This was a shifting point that brought balance back into my life. Breaking away so many of my bad habits, I was free to be hooked to the heart of Father God and wanted to pursue everything the Holy Spirit had to offer."

~Danielle

I simply love the way God can put us in exactly the places we need to be, at exactly the time we need it. He can use even our reluctant obedience to navigate us to a place of freedom. To come out of the critical levels of a spiritual lack, I must breathe in the life-support of the Kingdom, the Word, and the Father's presence through worship. Here I watch as He turns the circumstances into an advantage. This is where my unbalance becomes beautiful, for this is the place that I truly saw God as God and me as not. This is the place the King of kings and my Heavenly Father can come in and create my adventure. He truly is *so very good* and speaks through the unbalance!

My Child,

I come to you in the moments of misunderstanding; when the world is feeling unbalanced, confusing, and every stable thing seems to be slipping through your fingers, I come to you and bring revelation and hope in the shift. See with my heart, from My perspective, and embrace this change. It is those moments of feeling like everything has settled into a comfortable rhythm that I entice you to the next level of your destiny. Comfort is the greatest enemy of progress. I want to propel you into the next level of understanding, breakthrough, and promise by asking you to step out of your predictability and entice you with more and more. Understand that most big changes in your life often lead to the next assignment. Be free to become beautifully unbalanced as you trust Me with renewed depth.

To be loved with full abandonment is to come unbalanced from anything you knew was possible. This is how I love you. In order to step into the fullness of the DNA I placed inside you and reach your greatest potential, I require you to become unbalanced from who you thought you were. You will become unbalanced as you walk out a radical, relationship-centered faith, as you leave behind the logical and step into the impossible. I will stretch your understanding of what once seemed like fiction to the miraculous wonder of what can be a reality. The deeper you dig into My Word, and the more passionately you believe it, you will feel the unbalance of loosing what you thought you knew for the experience and knowledge that I am the originator of the mystical. I Am!

I do not guarantee a lack of turbulence, but I do promise to give you wisdom and perspective. You pray for new vision and mountain top moments, so do not grow faint as I fly you to these new levels. As the plane of potential ascends, so will it feel like your stomach is in knots and your heart is pounding excessively. Trust the process. Trust Me. The journey you started as you entered this world was preordained to be just that, a journey. I am the great navigator and will lead you through deep valleys and to the marvel at the pinnacle. Allow yourself to find peace amid the high and lows of life. I am your safe place and unwavering tower. Like a lighthouse in a storm, look for My light to find your way through the distance.

*In the unbalance, you may stumble, but you **will** regain your steadiness. In the unbalance, you may fall, but you will not stay down. In the unbalance, you may break to pieces, but you will be restored, more stunning than before. Your unbalance is beautiful to Me because it means you are living! So, live my child! Live like there is no tomorrow. Live like you have something to prove. Live like you cannot fail. Live like you genuinely believe that I created a radical destiny to step into. Get uncomfortable, keep dreaming, keep believing, keep living. Your living shines My glory for all the world to see! You are an example for others to follow. Be brave, for the most wondrous breakthroughs come after moments of unbalance.*

You are so radically loved that I created the greatest unbalance of all, just for you. Jesus came to Earth to defeat death, but in order to do so had to be crucified, die, and be buried. On the third day in the tomb, the greatest unbalance of all humanity occurred. He rose from the dead! Resurrection power proving the ultimate victory of Heaven on Earth. I apply this same life-giving power to those who believe. Step into the fullness of life I have always wanted you to have. When you call, I will answer!

You do not need to have it all together because I love you beautifully unbalanced. I love you from My beginning to the never ending.

Your Father, your Friend, your I AM!

CHAPTER TEN
VICTORY

"The horse is made ready for the day of battle, but the victory belongs to the Lord."
Proverbs 21:31 (NIV)

"But thanks be to God, who gives us the victory through our Lord Jesus Christ."
I Corinthians 15:57 (NKJV)

"For everyone who has been born of God overcomes the world. And this is the victory that has overcome the world—our faith."
I John 5:4 (ESV)

"For the LORD your God is the one who goes with you to fight for you against your enemies to give you victory."
Deuteronomy 20:4 (NIV)

"The LORD appeared to us in the past, saying: "I have loved you with an everlasting love; I have drawn you with loving-kindness."
Jeremiah 31:3 (NIV)

History is made by a person willing to step out of average and into extraordinary. For those in connection to God, there is no fear in this step because we trust He can orchestrate each step. Looking in the Bible, so many unlikely candidates shifted their narrative and, accordingly, history as we know it. This happened because they were eager to be used outside of their comfort zones.

Jesus gathered twelve outsiders and nobodies (from the world's perspective) and changed the world. David was delivering food when he entered a sword fight with a rock, and whose victory there led to him to becoming a king. Noah was considered a drunk who built a boat in the desert and saved all life, as we know it. Moses was adopted and had an identity crisis, which led to him to murder. Through stuttering words, he set God's people free from slavery. John the Baptist was a bug-eating, crazy person who was actually the only person who knew what they were talking about.

Victory does not come through filtered perfection but giving life your all, the good and the bad. Sometimes, the Lord wants to do something *through* us, illuminating the authority He placed in us. Other times, He wants to do something *for* us, to emphasize our sonship and our Kingdom connection. The way to recognize which victory we are experiencing or about to step into is by truly seeking God. When I seek my Father in Heaven, whether in the secret place, through worship, devotional, prayer, fasting, or asking Him for more of Himself, He will grant it every time. Then, when I come from that intimate time, I am rewarded by Him in public, which can transform everything.

In this way, I can live without stress because my Father is always with me. It is irrelevant what the circumstances look like if I have "sweet victory in Jesus."[27] From a Christian perspective, we should also see victory in the defeat because in the defeat, there is an opportunity for resurrection. True victory comes not from winning, but ascending to new levels of truth. When Christ died, He was "defeated," and it seemed the Devil had won. ***But*** when Christ arose from the dead, He

---

[27] (Bartlett 1939)

brought true victory that could not be gained by eternal life. Rather, it was by conquering that which thought it had power over Him that established for all eternity the ultimate truth— that nothing, including death, could defeat our Almighty God. The living power of Christ is greater than *all* forces on Earth and in every spiritual arena.

In chess, players move their pawns around the board, dominating the opposing team's pieces until they capture the most important piece, the king. The opponent tries to maneuver his pieces to get the king into a vulnerable place of imminent defeat, at which point they issue a "check." The king then must strategize a move that gets him out of this spot; otherwise, it becomes a checkmate, and he is defeated.

I got a beautiful picture as I was driving of the game chess in the context of our lives. So many of us have been, or currently are in, situations of feeling pinned down. We have arrived in a place, either spiritually or physically, that we feel like life is screaming "check" or "checkmate." There is a scramble to try and strategize or explain a way out of the situation. I hear the Lord saying, *"There is victory in the defeat!"* Not in giving up on life, but in turning everything over to God and trusting Him and Him alone to resurrect solutions, where you saw none. Give up the game you have been playing and step into the reality of the more. Any sacrifice of understanding will be met with an explosion of truth, hope, and revelation. There is honor here that will create sustainable triumph in all arenas of existence.

***

Beth is amazing in the vulnerability she expresses when telling her astounding story of victory. It was not a clear-cut path for her, and mistakes were made. Despite this, one truth is solid; God's love is so big, so personal, and so incredibly good!

"Being the daughter of a preacher, I've known the Lord for a long time. Despite this, I went 'off the reservation' for a long time. When I came back, the Lord was already speaking to me in different ways.

I will start at the very beginning of how my "road to Damascus" moment happened all in one evening.

I had joined the military, and it was difficult in this new community to find a church, especially one that was charismatic. My husband grew up Catholic and had more of a religious background than a relationship with God. This caused him to not really understand who God was. I knew how great God was and the tangible way He could show up in any circumstances. We had moved around and been through several churches. At the time of this 'wow, God moment,' we were living in North Carolina.

It was around August of 2013, and I felt like the Lord was saying, 'It's time to get out of the Marine Corps.' This was incredibly shocking because I only had five years until retirement. To me, this request had zero logic to it. I had worked my way into a position of authority and had sixty-three Marines who worked for me, and just finished running a group of 243. I had a lot going on, and I loved what I was doing. I wanted to be obedient, however, so I prayed about it and even went down for an altar call to have my pastor pray for me.

Fast forward to early October. I felt the Lord say, Submit.' He was telling me to submit to my boss. I understand that most people are like, 'Why were you not submitted to your boss?' Why would the Lord have to tell you that?' I have worked for many bosses, and to get in that position, you have to know how to delegate. There is a difference, though, between delegating and abdicating. The boss that I was supposed to submit to had abdicated all responsibility for his job. Unless it brought glory to him in some way, I had all the responsibilities—literally everything. I responded to the Lord, out loud in my car, 'I don't even know how to do that. I do not know what you are asking me to do. That makes absolutely no sense.' There was no response, except the need to submit just kept filling my spirit. Father did not elaborate more. He just told me what I needed to do in a very straightforward manner.

My stubborn nature won going even into November, and I still would not submit. He was even doing this to my team, and I could not have that. He had already been reprimanded and told he needed to do his job. It came to a head between my boss and me. I told him all the things that I thought he needed to hear, probably without a spoonful of sugar, and had even gone over his head to my other enlisted boss and told him what was going on.

Without my knowing, he was lying in wait for the day that I did not submit. When that day came, he completely played it off. Two weeks passed, and I had worked over a twelve-hour day when he pulled me into his office as I was leaving. To my dismay, he gave me what is called a NIP lock. It is a non-punitive letter of caution, basically a piece of paper that says, if you ever do this again, I will bring charges against you. I was absolutely crushed. I gave all my loyalty to my job, and this is what I got in return. I went home devastated. It felt like I was rolled down a hill and escalated out of my control.

I picked up my grandmother, and as we drove home, I decided I was not going to talk about getting this NIP lock. That night, however, a Staff Sergeant got drunk and was acting out in his front yard, to the point of pulling out a gun. He was from a squadron that was about to deploy with MEU (a Marine Expeditionary Unit) on a ship. They kicked him off the next day. Now needing a replacement, my boss, who had just reprimanded me, said, 'I got just the person.' So not only did I get this NIP lock the night before, but then in one swoop, I got relieved of my shop. This included the sixty-three Marines who I oversaw. All of it was taken away, and I was sent down to the MEU. What was even more infuriating was that the Staff Sergeant who had caused all the issues went back to the squad and did not even get in any trouble.

The reason MEU was so traumatizing was that, following the Thanksgiving we were heading into, we were going to deploy for three weeks. I would be gone most of December. Then when we came back, we would deploy again for nine months come February. I was blown away because I had a small daughter. My husband and I were both in the Marines, and we were not set up to handle this. It was like looking at my life in a snow globe, and it had just shattered.

My whole world was shifting so rapidly; I could scarcely comprehend what was happening. I cried out to God and felt Him say in my spirit, 'You didn't submit.' It was not that the Lord was punishing me, but He had lovingly given me a forewarning, and I chose not to listen.

I went to pick up my grandmother for Thanksgiving. As we drove, I kept thinking that I must tell her what was going on. After I finally broke down and did, she said, 'No, you're not! You are not going next week. You're not going on that deployment, and I'm just going to pray you out right now.' I argued back that I could not get out yet because I was five years away from retirement, and it did not make sense. She shot back, 'I'll just pray you into an early retirement.' Audacity took over, I guess, because I jumped on board. We had the pastor over to pray, and we all fasted through Thanksgiving.

When I went back to work on Monday, we had an aircraft that broke down and could not make it to the boat. There were two avionics people fixing it, but they needed to launch the boat. I had the training necessary, so I told them to go launch, and I would finish fixing it. I fixed that aircraft and launched it out. After I got it fixed, I got a call from my new Master Gunnery Sergeant.

This man stood about six-foot-four inches and was very intense and abrupt. It was the same Master Gunner who had been adamant that I would come to the boat, do the workup, and integrate into the team. In the phone call, he said, 'Since you fixed it, just get your stuff in order so we can leave in February. You're good to go.' In an instant, I became awesome in his book. I went home, and we celebrated the answered prayer of getting me out of the first deployment, but also kept our eyes fixed on what to do about the imminent date in February.

Eventually, I took my grandmother home, a three-hour, easy trip. On the way back, I was on the phone with my girlfriend, and we were consumed talking about all the different Holy Spirit experiences we were each having. Suddenly, a billboard caught my attention as it flashed, 'Pay attention and make the right turn.' I felt like it was a God note and quickly thought, 'I'm trying to make the right choice.' I continued talking to my friend when I saw that same billboard, and it flashed again. This time I was a little bitter, 'Lord, I'm trying!' My friend and I could only talk for a minute more before the call dropped, and I could not get her back.

I sat driving in silence and saw a billboard for cowboy boots, which is not a common thing in North and South Carolina. My daughter had wanted some cowgirl boots for Christmas, so I tried to memorize which exit it was. I drove on down the road, and I could not for the life of me remember what the exit number was. I tried to make an educated guess, pick an exit, and get off. I felt like I was supposed to turn left, and the store would be on my immediate left. After doing that, I realized that I guessed wrong, and I had turned into a residential area in the middle of nowhere.

As I drove along trying to get unlost, I saw a church, and the first sign I saw was, 'Christ Church -A Place for You.' Then another sign flashed up, saying, 'Come on in!' The parking lot was packed out of this huge church, so much so that people were parked in the grass. I felt like this was an invitation from God, but it was not good timing. I may have argued some, but the Lord is so gracious with us in our moments of haughty indignation and still desires us to make the appointment with Him.

I still had to turn back around because I realized that I was not in the right place. In the process of turning around, I thought, 'If you want me to go in there, Lord, You are going to have to give me a sign.' As I pulled through the lot, there was a sign that said, 'Majestic Cuts,' on a separate little church that had a purple mantle running through it. That caught my attention and sounded interesting, but I decided if I was going in, the sign had to be bigger than that. I got turned around and saw the flashing sign again, and it said, 'Come in, and celebrate with us!'

I thought, 'Okay, Lord, I got it, You want me to come in here, and that's fine, but Lord, I am not parking in the grass here. This is a big church, I don't attend here, and I'm looking like a hot mess, so You'll have to give me a parking space right down front if You want me to go in.' As I drove back around, I couldn't believe what I saw. I was like, 'Oh, you have got to be kidding me!' Right by the doors was a spot just for me.

*I headed into this church, rocking some spandex. My hair was a mess and up; I had no makeup on, and I was in tennis shoes. I walked in, and this church was **huge**. You could fit my entire home church in their foyer. They even had a fancy barista. Looking around, I got the sense it was like a cantata or some type of Christmas musical. I kept walking and let an usher seat me since it was extremely dark. As I was trying to get my eyes to adjust, a little group of kids came onto the stage and began talking.*

The first little girl to speak said, 'I'm gluten intolerant. I am allergic to this, and I cannot eat that. I cannot do this.' I made a humorous connection to my friend Rachel, who I was just on the phone with because she has many of the same issues. In my head, I chuckled to myself, thinking, 'Hey, what's Rachel doing here?'

As they continued talking, I panned over because there was light coming from the corner. There was a big life vest hanging, and it had words on it that read, USS Majestic. This captured my attention like a hit to the heart because I was supposed to go on a USS Baton in February and the majestic connection from the 'Majestic Cuts' sign I had just seen outside. The Lord sweetly whispered, 'Do you hear Me now? Do you see where you are now?'

As I watched this program, completely engrossed now, I realized this little group of kids were on a cruise ship. They had a coordinator who was taking them through and telling me about the sights they were going to see and activities they were going to participate in. As they were talking, this group of friends found out that they were all Christians, but one. They began to minister to her and started telling her about Jesus. Then came three little penguins, standing over by the USS Majestic. They chimed in, 'Humans always make things so complicated. They are always overthinking everything. They are always worried about everything. The Lord loves us so much that even living in a frozen tundra, He will feed us, and we do not have to worry about anything. So, how much more will He care for His children?'

That exact scripture had been on my heart, and I had been praying it over and over. Matthew 6:25-27 (NIV)

> "Therefore I tell you, do not worry about your
> life, what you will eat or drink; or about your
> body, what you will wear. Is not life more than
> food, and the body more than clothes? Look at
> the birds of the air; they do not sow or reap or
> store away in barns, and yet your heavenly

Father feeds them. Are you not much more valuable than they? Can any one of you by worrying add a single hour to your life?"

At first, as these God moments took place and I felt God's love hit my heart, I was crying, but only little tears. Then the penguins pushed me over the edge, and I was snot nose crying. I am sure these people did not know what to think of me. I spoke to the Lord in my spirit, 'Got it, Lord! Whether I get deployed, or I don't; however it works out, You have got the whole thing; I trust You, and I'm okay.' A song broke out, and the backdrop lit up. I thought that I was ugly crying already, but apparently, the Lord still had more work to do.

As this backdrop was illuminated, I noticed it was a huge ship. Like, bigger-than-your-house, huge. As I took it all in, I realized it was not a cruise ship but a silhouette of an LHD, which was the type of ship that I was supposed to be going on. Sobbing, in a random church, in a random town in South Carolina, my Father in Heaven met me and injected into my very being that I was going to be fine.

The Lord orchestrated to have a cantata with a ship and those darn adorable penguins speaking to me in the scripture that I had been praying. You just do not get any bigger than that! It is in these insanely huge, beyond comprehension moments that we can see victory, even while still walking out the storm.

I eventually made it home and more supernatural events aligned that allowed me to retire early. Wanting to leave with honor and not just ditch, they even allowed my husband to volunteer for the nine-month deployment I was expected to go on. God is so amazing and willing to shower us with His love in the most unlikely of ways.

Since then, I have been passionately following God via Holy Spirit. Where He leads, I follow and have been (and continue to) be used in mighty ways for His glory. There is absolute victory when you follow the prompting of God, even to a place of finding victory in the defeat."

~Beth

God loves you with an everlasting love. So, if you have not picked up on this concept yet, please pause and let it sink in. *God loves you!* Not with just any conditional, temporary, fictitious, fantasy, demanding kind of love, but a draw-you-in-with-loving-kindness kind of love. It would entice you, charm you, fascinate you, and attract you because it is so pleasing in its authenticity. That love is the characteristic of being everlasting, meaning it cannot fade, wash off, distort, change its mind, alter, dilute, or cancel out. It is *eternal.* God is love, and from God's beginning until the never ending, He has and always *will* love you. There is victory in this love. It will meet us in unlikely places and give us answers to questions we did not know how to ask yet. Our Heavenly Father is so passionate about us that He wants us to experience Him before we even have the capacity to understand the experience.

***

There is a simplicity to our battle strategy to gain victory in our lives, and it simply begins with a sacrificial "Yes." Jesus did not overcomplicate His mission when He came to Earth, both fully God and fully man, to be the living example of love and victory. As our next amazing individual, Cristi, says, God simply "loved the hell right out of her." As her story graces these pages, she can testify to the reality of this concept radically changing her life.

"I grew up in a dysfunctional home and was completely bound in rejection. I was trapped in addiction for over twenty years, including thirteen years of being a meth head on the streets of Amarillo, Texas. I knew there was a god, somewhere, far away, but not one that loved me. I did not ever think I could be good enough to be a part of Him or know Him.

I met a man named Brad in 2000, started dating him, and within three months moved in with him. Little did I know that this man's mother would be the channel through which God would change my life.

Dolores had been through quite a bit in her life, including being radically set free from a thirteen-year homosexual lifestyle. At the time of this story, she had just been born again and ended up in Red River, New Mexico. Also, at this time, I was living with her son; we were not married and very much living in sin. Brad and I were both using drugs, even though prior to meeting me, he had never done anything like that. I pulled him in with me because, as the saying goes, 'misery loves company.' I would love to tell you that I had gotten clean for my kids, but I did not. I had three daughters in the mess of the meth addiction. (I must be honest to show you the miracle of Jesus.)

Suddenly, the Lord spoke to her on March 3, 2003, and said, 'Dolores, I need you to move to Amarillo.' Without totally knowing why, but with total faith, she followed the Lord to Texas. With this being such a sudden move, we knew that she needed a place to stay. There really was not even a discussion about it; we knew she had to stay with us. All-in-all, she stayed about two weeks.

We had only met once before, but now I was pregnant. Her son, Brad, and I had lost two babies before this pregnancy, but alas, that did not slow my meth addiction. In addition to the drugs, I was also very much into witches, spell books, tarot cards, palm reading, and horoscopes. That whole world had drawn me in because I felt a false sense of power and control there. Then, in comes Brad's mom, a spirit-filled believer, who stayed two weeks and then left.

Since I was not married to her son, she had full spiritual authority in our house. Knowing this, she simply commanded the darkness out and asked God's light to come in. She anointed the trailer house and blessed us. She did not take out my worldly stuff or condemn us in our sin. She just loved us right where we were, having full faith in God to do the rest. She prayed over our home and broke the power of darkness in my life. That is how I came to know who Jesus was before I even knew His name. I literally had no understanding of life. Being a drug addict for so long, you lose all sense of reality. I did not know that Easter was about Jesus until I was 28 years old. I remember during 9/11 waking up with all the horror that was taking place and thinking, 'What is a terrorist?' That is how far removed I had become that I could not comprehend even the world around me.

Fast forward a few months, and I ended up delivering our daughter, Ashley. I went right back to meth after having the baby. Within six months of Dolores coming to stay with us, something supernatural happened. I came home one day, walked in the door, and Brad immediately met me saying,

'We can't do this...' and I finished his sentence 'anymore. We can't do this.' I knew at that moment that I could not do meth anymore. There was not an ultimatum given, no threat to stop, nothing. There was no reason in the world for me to agree with him to quit. It had been a part of me for thirteen years, but at that moment, I had something in me that said I must stop doing this.

I locked myself up in our trailer house while Brad continued to go to work. My girls, Brianna and Ashley, were with me, and I stopped cold turkey. It felt like an unseen force was helping me. I did not know what it was because I was so naive when it came to spiritual things. Unexpectedly, in addition to losing the desire for drugs, I also let go of my artificial spiritual attachments. I never looked at another Ouija board again. I didn't get rid of it; I just was never drawn to anything I had previously been drawn to.

To say it was easy would be a lie. It was not. My life just became sleeping and eating to cope. Within four months or so, I got sober. I never relapsed and never went to rehab. I still had terrible addict dreams but I was still able to quit.

I was getting sober and becoming a natural human being. When something good happened, Brad's mom would say, 'That's a God thing.' Through these four simple words, I began to think, 'What is that? What does that mean?' She would say it about literally everything—from a raise to a $25 bonus (which was huge to us because we had nothing, so every small thing was attributed to God). Over time she began to soften my heart.

It had been about six months from stopping cold turkey when we took my oldest daughter, Brianna, to a *birthday party. It was held at a sweet little church that had a cool recreation room. Just as we walked in, Brad grabbed my arm and said, 'You think we need to go to church?' My instant response, without even fully knowing why, was to say, 'That's a God thing.'*

We went to Dolores' house right after dinner and announced to her we were going to go to church with her. Two weeks before, she had gotten a prophetic word saying she would be raising her hands and praising the Lord for who would be beside her. It was crazy because that next Sunday, we were in church with her. So, whenever I walked into that church and realized the goodness and shift I had felt was Holy Spirit, I was all in. Then I met Jesus and learned what He had done for me; I was a sold-out yes.

As I sat through that service, I recognized the feeling or presence of what had helped me when getting sober. I could instantly identify that sense of goodness and strength as soon as I walked into the building. I did not know it at the time, but I could feel the love of God and Holy Spirit.

A pastor, Robert Morris, was preaching that week; he did a salvation call, and I gave my life to Jesus. It was June 13, 2004, and I have never turned back. Since then, I have been all in, sold out, done. Making such a radical transformation was not effortless, but it has been 100% worth it. The Lord began to show me what He had done to capture my heart. He came and met me right where I was. I always tell people, 'There is not a religious bone in my body because I came straight from the streets.' I encountered Jesus Christ, the real King of kings, and that was it. I did not know the language or theology through which to filter anything. It was just raw, real Jesus chasing after me.

After saying yes to the Lord, Brad and I ended up moving from our tiny trailer into a large house that was big enough to invite Dolores to live with us. This was God created because it allowed a situation that kept me from going back. She came alongside me and discipled me through deliverance to a place of wholeness. She sat with Jesus, day in and day out for years, for me. She loves to tell people she 'loved the hell out of me.' Now, following in her example, that is what I do. People come to church, and they get touched, have a radical experience, and feel the Lord, but then there is no one to catch them when they start to go the wrong way. The Lord showed me that I was so very important to Him in so many radical ways.

Years later, God showed me that from the very beginning of my life, I was just a hurt, lost girl trying to find my way. The meth was just the last thing I picked up that made me feel found. I always tell people that are dealing with addiction or parents that have children battling addiction, 'It's really not that big of a deal.' When Jesus gets involved, there is no chain that He cannot break, or heart too far gone to love them into His embrace. The world tries to make addiction something you can never get free of or something you will be forced to battle your whole life, and I believe that's a lie.

I eventually became a mentor for addicts through some different organizations. I would get these girls, and they would do great for a stretch but eventually would return to addiction. I was like, 'Lord, I know, you took it from me, why are these girls failing?' He reminded me how I had been discipled and the importance of discipleship. It is so important because it can sustain the work the Lord is doing.

On top of mentoring, shortly after being saved, I began to hear, 'Yes, Lord' everywhere. When I would go to church, someone would say it on the other side of the sanctuary, and it would be so loud, I would have to hold my ears. It was like they were screaming it every time I heard it. Despite what I thought were a list of shortcomings, I began to have visions while driving. I would see people wearing black t-shirts that said, 'Yes Lord' in a certain script. One day, while I was with Dolores, I explained about hearing 'Yes Lord' and seeing people wearing the shirts, and even about seeing myself handing them out. When I told her this that day, she turned white.

She took me to a Bible in her room that she was using in 1999. (I did not meet Brad till 2001.) She had just been set free and was writing to the Lord. She had paused in her journaling, and in the middle of a blank space, the Lord said, 'I need you to write Yes Lord.' As we looked at this scribbling, it was the exact script as the t-shirts I saw in my visions. That day we both knew we would have a ministry.

We ended up waiting ten years because we thought we needed to have God hand us a ministry. Eventually, the structure for this ministry evolved from a Holy Spirit centered worship night that I experienced with my daughter. There was a gathering with worship and an opportunity to soak in the presence of the Lord. I knew as I sat there and felt the Spirit move, the shirts were a part of this. So, I took the money I had set aside, and with the exact amount down to pennies, I stepped out in faith and bought 28 shirts. I anointed, and I prayed over every one of them. I felt like the Lord had said, 'If you will give away the shirts, I'll do the rest.'

Our first 'Yes Lord' night was August 30, 2015, in my house. My sister, who is a network marketer, put on her shirt and posted on social media, 'I'm with you, sister.' That night we went global. People began to message with orders for shirts. It is simply a ministry of obedience. Now we have given approximately 4,500 shirts away, all over the world with stories to match.

In one story, the shirts supernaturally multiplied in Uganda this past year. A friend of mine took 225 shirts for staff and children. After she gave them away to all 200+ individuals, they still had over 100 in the back of the van, and she does not know how, to this day. I do not know how many people believe that stuff, but I believe anything is possible with God.

A businessman was having breakfast with his assistant, who was wearing a 'Yes Lord' shirt. He had been praying for an open door to reach the youth in Kenya. He had a heart to preach the Gospel but needed a miracle to make it happen. During the breakfast, a man walked up to the gentlemen, looked at the assistant's shirt, and said, 'What Lord are you saying yes to?' This simple interaction opened the door for this man. He went home, packed his things, and moved to Kenya. Here, the Lord opened the door for him to reach and influence the youth in 6,000 different churches. I had another guy who stole his shirt out of his dad's closet and ended up taking himself to rehab.

We have gotten multiple women who had issues getting pregnant and were healed after wearing the shirts. We call the product of this, 'Yes babies.' Absolutely amazing stories like that, all surrounded around a simple t-shirt.

It obviously is not the actual shirt that is causing the amazing testimonies that are following them. It is the prayer and anointing that is on the shirt—the faith to step out and simply be a child of God. The Lord can work in mysterious ways. Sometimes it is something as simple as a shirt that can love us to a place of redefining or fully committing to the 'yes' in our heart."

~Cristi

When was the last time you "loved the hell out of someone?" What a beautiful model to live our life by. The way that God can take our mess and transform it into a wondrous masterpiece leaves me in humbled awe. He, in turn, is not only setting us free from ourselves but giving us a powerful testimony. We then have the capacity to set others free from the same chains that previously held us captive. This is one way we can discover how God wants to use us to influence the world.

Our sphere of influence, also referred to as the Greek word *"metron,"*[28] comes alive as we simultaneously impact the world and find the fullness of joy by walking out our purpose. It is the "boundaries" or "limited portion" that helps direct us to the specific door that God designed just for us. It is our fingerprint that is needed to open it, causing an effect that leaves the world better than it was without us. The sphere which God appointed to us is where He expects us to take responsibility within—not overextending or for the purpose of boasting, but for the glory of God.

It is amazing to me that not only did He create us in His image, loves us with an intentional passion, designed us for

---

[28] (Wilkins 2009)

greatness, with unique, special traits and talents, but He also created a niche in the world that only we have the capacity to fill.

Our Father in Heaven wants life to be enjoyable and exciting, so this niche is not the completion of a chore list to begrudgingly take on. Rather, this niche is discovering our true, redeemed heart's desires and walking them out with the anointing of our Heavenly Father. To pinpoint what area our niche might be, you can look at the highlight reel of our life and discover where favor was received. How did you feel in different environments? What was the solution or answer you needed when you were lost or before you even realized what the question was? What misfortunes do you see in the world that you wish you could be part of the solution? What gifts and talents have the Father blessed you with? All these answers lace together to create your sphere of influence. To be honest, I am still trying to figure this out.

The connecting of my talents with my heart, weaving it into the passion projects the Lord has ignited in my spirit, and combining them with the place favor has always ignited in my life has yet to lead me to something specific, but this does not mean I have given up seeking and praying. Quite the contrary. I am faithful to where my Father has placed me and diligent in the tasks He has assigned for me. I want to honor these seeds of opportunity with a spirit-filled work ethic to allow God to grow them to the point of producing His holy fruit.

A verse I live by and even have tattooed on my arm says, *"Whatever you do, work at it with all your heart, as working for the Lord, not for human masters,"* Colossians 3:23 (NIV). I do not have to worry about growing roots and being faithful in the "now" for fear of "getting too comfortable." The Great Creator is also the God of transplanting and can move me whenever and wherever He desires. This book is one of my biggest leaps into the unknown. I am trusting Holy Spirit to guide me through unknown territory as we cultivate and create the answer, the answer I wish I had as a born-again believer, the answer to questions I did not know how to ask or seek, the answers I did not know existed. My prayer is that in some small way, this book gives you hope, answers questions, and activates a dialogue of intrigue with your Heavenly Father.

Whatever life throws at you, wherever you are at this very moment, there is victory in the *now* to propel you to the horizon. What will you place your focus on? It is so important to visualize your victory; see it to believe it. As believers, we should know the power of putting faith in something before it becomes tangible. Setting our eyes, hopes, and hearts on the future before it unfolds allows us to prepare the way. We cannot simply sit back and wait for our victory to fall in our lap, but be active and engaged in partnering with God to unveil the triumph.

My Child,

*I am a promise-keeping God, and victory is a promise I keep. I desire **all** of you, my sweet child. Your forfeit of self does not mean defeat, but rather it brings forth the triumphant victory I have predestined for **you**. Let My Spirit rain down on you and soothe your troubled heart! As you stand in the storm, seek Me as I reveal the keys to the future— these keys that will unlock the doors you have yet been allowed to fully walk through.*

I am unconventional, so My logic and wisdom will not fit into the comprehension of man. This box that you try to place Me in was created by you, a creation that you thought would make life feel safe. So, I call to you to redesign your box. Allow Me to be your walls of safety, your healing embrace, and your secret place as I whisper and speak peace to you when the world gets far too overwhelming. The volume around you seems to soothe your spirit, but this is a crutch you long ago outgrew.

So, stand with me in the hush, the still quiet of this new day. The dew is still sticking to the grass in cleansing anticipation of what the future holds. There is so much more than you have given yourself credit for. Allow yourself the freedom to trust Me. Your "what if" is being transformed. It is a "what if" that walks away from anxiety and fear of the unknown and steps into joyful anticipation of what I am about to do, with full faith that it is good!

There is still an enemy trying to defeat you and crippled you with plot twists. Stop giving him the pen to write your story. Stop letting him fill you with fear of shadows and ghosts of the past. Stop looking back and see what is facing forward!

I am taking back the pen to inscribe on your heart a foreword of inspiring hope. See what I am creating. The harvest is coming from seeds planted in seasons past. Do not get so distracted by how the seeds were planted that you miss the splendor of the fruit.

You are not a statistic; you are My unique treasure, a testimony of courage, victory, faith, intentionality, and joy! There's more here, and we will unearth the pieces that need to breathe, bury those that need to be laid to rest, and prune that which the lack of attention is causing unhealthy growth.

*Gentle was not promised; fair was not promised; easy was not promised. **Love** was promised. **Relationship** was promised. **Power** and **authority** were promised through My ultimate sacrifice. Everything I do is orchestrated to bring you back to Me because **I love you**.*

I love seeing the world through your eyes, the magnificence and wonder of every piece, the way you light up at the thought of Me, and the special, precious moments I send your way throughout your day. The way the Spirit explodes out of you is changing the atmosphere and breaking the chains around you. I am obviously around you, through you, and in you, so be bold in your blessings, for they are original! With everything you have, worship Me! With total abandonment, let My glory rain down on you!

Love you into more and more,
your Father, Comfort, Victor, and your Biggest Fan

CHAPTER ELEVEN
LOVE'S GOT A LOT TO DO WITH IT!

Shout joyfully to the Lord, all the earth; Break forth and sing for joy and sing praises.
Psalm 98:4 (NASB)

My heart, O God, is steadfast; I will sing and make music with all my soul. Awake, harp and lyre! I will awaken the dawn. I will praise you, LORD, among the nations; I will sing of you among the peoples. For great is your love, higher than the heavens; your faithfulness reaches to the skies. Be exalted, O God, above the heavens; let your glory be over all the earth.
Psalm 108:5 (NIV)

Music has always been such a lifeline to my spirit as I discovered the tangible, expressive love of my Heavenly Father. It has such amazing health benefits such as decreasing anxiety, improving mood, assisting with pain relief, and creating opportunities for powerful emotional expression. There's no doubt that music can have a positive physical, mental, and spiritual influence. Different songs have resonated throughout my life with joyful intensity, like my own personal soundtrack, giving hope, direction, motivation, or faith when I needed it most. Worship can infiltrate the most mundane of moments with the perfect song and speak the words that felt so impossible to articulate. Most recently, the lyrics from the song *Now I See*, by Paul and Hannah

McClure[29] spoke to my heart of Father's radical, relentless love for me in a beautifully tangible way.

Eye's wide open to be able to see, was a verbal illustration that still echoes like a gong in my heart and makes my spirit leap for joy. The testimony that goes behind those simple words is my very own miracle. The Almighty God saw an angry teen searching for answers and led me on a journey that was anything but obvious at the time. I ran smack into the love of a God I was trying to disprove because of a sacrifice I could not receive. Now, I walk with a Holy Spirit that once seemed like fiction. I have embodied the power of reconciliation that brings life—a life that I literally could not trade for the world.

***

There are times that we go searching for God and other times God chases us down and wins our hearts in a miraculous way. As a representative of both, Kathy speaks to the miracle of life, the possibility of the impossible, and God's beautiful grace, as she shares with us her powerful testimony. She knows first-hand that it's in those moments of "not okay", that we become desperate enough to "let go and let God".

"My husband, Robert, and I agree, our greatest miracle was the birth of our daughter Alli. We had never experienced God's love in such a powerful, tangible way until that moment. She was an answered prayer for me. I do not think my husband even knew my heart's desire at that time or that I was praying to get pregnant. God is so beyond our

---

[29] (McClure and McClure 2019)

understanding and comprehension and yet loves us in our imperfection.

We were just dating at the time, serious but not planning on getting married anytime soon. Despite what I know now about the importance of being married, God still blessed us with an answered prayer.

Everything started with me going to the doctor because I was having 'lady problems,' including a significant amount of pain. He diagnosed me, but I forget what they called it. The doctor informed me that I would never have children. There was scar tissue building up on my fallopian tubes that had no real explanation. Even with an operation, there would only be a small chance for pregnancy because of the limitations it created. The fallopian tubes would be filled with irreparable damage, and I would not be able to conceive at all.

I was devastated walking out of that office. I was not even thinking about kids at that time in my life. The reality of never be able to have them made me not even feel like a woman. I told my husband (boyfriend at the time), and he seemed okay with it, trying to be strong for me. I was not okay with this, so I prayed.

It was not even a long time that I prayed. I started feeling sick again, so I went into the doctor's office, and they did a test. Sure enough, the test came back positive that I was pregnant! I was sitting on that bench there, so overwhelmed. I do not even think my feet hit the floor from the euphoria I was feeling. Walking out on a cloud nine, I began thinking, 'Oh, my God! Wow!' I was radically overwhelmed. I went from being told that 'you are not going to ever have kids' to seeing God's gift of love just for me! At that moment, my concept of God's goodness shifted.

He turned a hope into the fact that He is real when He answered my prayer. I remember vividly getting on my knees and declaring, 'Lord, this baby is yours!' The only way I knew to walk that out was to get connected with a church. Robert and I both had the Spirit in us, but we pushed it aside and were not living a Christian life. To be honest, we were doing quite a bit of drugs and stuff. This created fear within me that I was not worthy of such a blessing and gift. I never would want to hurt this life growing inside of me, so from that moment forward, I walked away from everything and offered myself as a pure temple to the Lord. Everything changed for me, and I just wanted to be in church all the time. I craved the presence of the Lord like a pregnancy craving.

Part of the beauty of this conception is that I did not consider it a healing but rather a gift just for me from God. Through the awesomeness of this life growing in me, I could feel the presence of God. I loved being pregnant because of the feeling of the baby growing. When I could feel the movement and kicking of life within me, the reality of how the Lord knits together life in the womb became so tangibly real. I had an overwhelming thankfulness to God within my heart, and I just wanted to serve Him by raising Alli.

The story of Hannah in 1 Samuel just kept resonating in my spirit. She could not have a baby, and then God did an awesome miracle. She dedicated her son, Samuel, to God. I, too, wanted to teach Alli about God, leave her in God's hands, and just thank God for her in every way that I could.

While Robert was not as overjoyed as me at first, He fell deeply in love with the life growing inside me quickly. I was a little bit scared about birth defects because of the lifestyle I had previously, but God blessed us with a healthy, vivacious bundle of love.

Robert is amazing with kids. The way he takes time with them and teaches them is amazing. He felt a responsibility, and I believe it was God pulling him into His heart. This great man and I were still immature as people ourselves; nevertheless, this overwhelming gift of love transformed us. We both were so focused on raising our child and pouring everything that we had into her, nothing else mattered anymore.

The doctor obviously was shocked and cautioned me from getting my hopes up for any more children. He explained the slim chance of this happening, all the medical reasons this should not have happened, and that it 'definitely' would not happen again. I knew in my spirit this was an answered prayer and believed that God was in charge and He could do the impossible. When I came in pregnant the second time and third time, I defied all medical logic. We started making the joke that I should get my money back for that first visit when the doctor set God up to show off. The nurses and doctors could not do anything but shake their heads and write me off as a miracle. I had never been 'healed,' scar tissue never disappeared, and the tests still showed this should not have happened to me. God, however, is not confined to the logic of man, for He is the Creator of life.

Robert and I came together with the same goal, and we loved these miracles so much. The whole time we were raising these kids, God kept drawing us closer to Him. It was through these beautiful lives that we came back to Him. The realization that there is no way that we wanted to do this on our own was obvious. I cannot remember how many times that we were so grateful that we were not doing life on our own, even in the moments that got overwhelming.

God had such an amazing plan that was so much bigger than us. Although we learned more later, deep down, we knew we should not be living together. I guess God sometimes can look past our faults and know the bigger picture. He knew that eventually, Robert and I would get married. Though, even if we did not, He designed these children, knit them together, and wanted their influence in the world. Grace does not allow us to sin but gives us the opportunity to grow and win.

As I came back to God, I started putting the pressure on Robert that we needed to get married. I almost was panicked because I wanted to raise my miracle right, and to do that, we needed to get married. (I now see it was fear of religion, rather than the love of God, operating in my heart.) Whenever I was doing that, though, Robert would start pushing me away, which would make me angry. After a while, I just let God's peace cover the situation, and we stayed busy raising our baby girl.

I stopped putting the pressure on and gave the situation to God. Even though I really wanted it to, that was not helping him heal. He had some heart trauma from his first marriage, and only time, combined with unconditional love, was going to restore him. Everyone's story is different, but seeking God's heart can bring wisdom to any situation.

It was Christmas when our first miracle was almost one. I think she was just pulling herself upon us as we opened our Christmas presents. Then that man of mine said, 'You missed one.' Here, he had put a little box in the Christmas tree. It was a ring, and much to my surprise, he proposed to me. We got married on Valentine's Day the following year and shortly after had our second miracle. We have gone through ups and downs, but no matter what, we did it together.

There is nothing more amazing than getting to see God go against all human odds and bring you your heart's desire. It did not matter what was medically 'possible' or whether our life was lined out perfect to be 'good enough' to be loved by God. The love of our Heavenly Father came in an unconditional package of joy and made us want to live a better life. God blessed us with a beautiful baby, who grew into a beautiful young lady who decided to write a powerful book."

~Kathy

Did you catch that? This is a testimony about me! I myself had only heard it for the first time when recording it for this book. I am that miracle baby. Kathy and Robert are my parents. As I processed this new revelation, understanding came in so many places. We can never fully understand someone unless we see the world through their eyes and hearts. This is why I love testimonies so much. As I sat and listened to my mom speak about the miracle of me, so much of my childhood and her parenting choices made sense. She may have dedicated me to the Lord before I was even born, but she had no parameters for what that would look like.

My whole life, I felt like an outsider, like I did not quite fit anywhere without majorly modifying my personality, likes, or beliefs. As I got older, there were people in high school who would throw parties but told me I could not go because I was "too good." There was a literal setting apart that, without parameters and understanding, left me feeling desperately isolated and alone. I had no idea what to do with this "goodness." I felt at a loss trying to cultivate it and grow in the identity and the confidence of the Lord.

Feeling lonely and misunderstood, I decided in college that I did not want to be "good" anymore and walked away from God. I pursued anything that made me feel powerful or seen. I took free will and exercised it to the full extent. Looking back, despite my free will, I can see the very distinct fingerprints of God throughout my life protecting me. This protective covering often felt like "bad-luck" or being "left out" or like "I couldn't get away with anything."

A perfect example took place in college. I was "all up in" my bad choices and destructive behavior. My best friend and I would hide in his car in the parking garage of our dorms and smoke weed. This was the early 2000s, so technology was just starting to explode on the scene. I was still sporting a "non-smart" cube of a Nokia cell phone. You know, the ones that only had that silly snake game on it, no camera, and you had to push real buttons to do anything? That ancient little phone would somehow manage to push enough buttons to call my mother while in my backpack. It never randomly dialed any other number, literally only my mother. She would get to hear all sorts of conversations of me in an altered state that no mother wants to hear. Now, this scenario would be bad enough if it happened once, but if you recall, I was not that "lucky." This crazy, illogical occurrence happened so much I started having to leave my phone behind. We still joke to this day that God was not going to let me get away with anything.

I had two reasons for being at college, to figure out what I wanted to do in life and prove that God did not exist. I signed up for several world religion classes, including witchcraft and paganism, to discover all the other options and thus disprove the "only way" concept. This did not go as planned because, after all my research and study, I simply proved to myself that God truly was the one true God and that Christ was who He claimed to be in scripture. The thing that solidified this for me boiled down to relationship.

In every other religion, you can know *of* the deity or prophet and follow their teachings and positive traditions, but none of them ever draw the believer in. There is a disconnect while trying to work hard enough, to be good enough, and find answers individually. God is the only deity that loves the believer so much He desires to do life in connection with them. He calls all of humanity His children and expresses an undeniable love for them. Christianity has mystical aspects that only a believer would understand but leave the follower with the hope that they are not alone.

It is stated in the Bible that Jesus desires us to become born again. This simply requires us to accept Him as our Lord and Savior, believe His perfect love, demonstrated through sacrifice, saved us, and ask Him to live within us[30]. This empowers us to live a life of connection. Though I eventually decided God was real, this made me furious. "If He is so real, why can't I experience Him?" The truth was that I was seeking to know *about* Him but not seeking to *know* Him. I was simply

---

[30] (BibleGateway n.d.)

too content in my anger to pursue Him. There would be many more years of hardship and running before I finally yielded to His outstretched arms of forgiveness and love.

We may not always understand why certain things are happening in our life, but if we trust God, He will reveal all in His perfect timing. God is the God of relationship, so how can that which we cannot see, be known? The Incarnate Deity wants us to walk with Him and experience all knowledge and wisdom. For this reason, He gives us the Bible. Many historians, Christian and non-Christian, have proved that the validity of the Bible is based on a range of different verifications. The Bible is made up of many writings, by a variety of authors from drastically different backgrounds, over a period of 1,500-2,000 years. Despite all these variances, the concept, heart, vision, intentionality, purpose, and details of God's Word never contradicts itself. It is self-consistent and extraordinarily authentic, which is truly a supernatural phenomenon. It has been confirmed by archeology and science many times over. It has made astonishing predictions of distant future events with flawless accuracy and has divine wisdom of the nature of the universe.

By making knowledge possible, a demonstration is made to prove the claim that the Bible is the Word of God. We recognize the voice of our Creator as He speaks through the thin pages of black, white, and red. The words come alive to Kingdom-minded believers. As they read, millions of people over the expanse of every continent have seen their lives radically changed by this powerful book. Based on this evidence, one must assume that these writings are "God-breathed" with His divine revelation.

In my passionate pursuit of God, I have experienced that He still speaks to us through writing in a beautiful and powerful way. I am in no way comparing this book to the divine Word that sets the standard of all standards. I am asking, though, if you are still skeptical, look at the evidence within these humble pages of the experiences from a variety of individuals with different backgrounds, meeting God in unique ways at diverse times in their life. There are countless individuals with these same influential encounters, far beyond what would fit between the covers of this book. The more evidence that is compounded, the greater the proof that this is far beyond coincidence and sits beautifully in the place of confirmation. Dare to step past the limited vantage point of logic and into the wide expanse of faith-based belief. For if God is the all-knowing, sovereign orchestrator of Heaven and Earth, how would my logic and understanding ever come close to His? There is beauty, peace, and hope when meditating on the bigness of God and His purposeful love for us individually.

***

On the wave of total infatuation with my Heavenly Father, this book could not end without the beautiful, passionate testimony of my unbelievable friend, Dawn. When I approached her about contributing her testimony to this book, she did not hesitate. Her zealous, fervent devotion to our God sets the bar for intimacy with the Alpha and Omega. She is madly in love with Jesus, and her life resonates with His authenticity and kindness.

"One fall Saturday night in a dim, pleasantly scented, oversized room flooded with green padded, interlocking seats, Jesus introduced Himself to me, and I've been hopelessly captivated with Him ever since. While my

relationship with Him began at that moment, His relationship with me started long beforehand. It began well before I accepted Him as my Lord and Savior, long before I heard about Him.

Before that fateful night, short of a few weddings and funerals (and a couple of other times I barely remember), I never saw the inside of a church. I knew one prayer, and it was about food. It was a prayer my grandparents said before meals when we were at their house. 'God is great. God is good. Let us thank Him for our food. Amen.'

For the most part, my family never prayed, talked about God or Jesus, or went to church. Strangely enough, though, when I was a young child, my mother taught my brothers and I a popular Sunday school song. The song was "Jesus Loves Me." We laughed and danced as we sang this song of a trustworthy and faithful God who was so huge and incomprehensible, yet who knew the little ones and protected them. It was just a song, but at the very same time, it was a seed—a seed Holy Spirit watered and nourished over the next three decades.

As an adult, I wanted to pursue a career in Corporate Training and Development. During the final years of my military service, I served in this field and loved it so much I wanted to pursue it afterward, so I sought out a Bachelor's degree to complement the years of experience I already possessed. I searched tirelessly for months to find a degree plan in this specific area. Hundreds of colleges and universities offered a degree program in Education but finding one that focused on Corporate Education and Training proved to be a difficult task. After almost a year of *searching, I finally found one school with a Corporate Training program—in a Christian university. Oh, poop.*

To say I was less than thrilled is an understatement. Church people never impressed me, and now I was considering spending hundreds of hours with them as I chased my dream. Since it was at a Christian university, this program also had some prerequisite courses related to the Old and New Testaments to graduate. All I could think was – 'BORING!' All things considered, though, these two 'strikes' were not enough to deter my registration, and I felt a small price to pay to get the degree I was looking for.

While taking classes, one of the better-paying companies in the area was hiring, and I applied for two jobs, one as a production technician, which I was exceptionally qualified for, and one in security, which I was much less qualified for. Although I barely met the position requirements, I was so excited to get a call from that company, and I received a job offer! Woohoo! 'But wait, security? Really?!' Yeah, that is what I thought too, but the pay was amazing, so I accepted the position.

I don't know if you know much about security and protection details, but you spend most of your time hoping nothing happens. So, after the initial training, I spent many, many hours in small, confined spaces with people who talked about God, family, church, baptisms, praying, what their preacher talked about last week, how God helped them through this dilemma, that catastrophe, and so much more. I did not know (at the time) how it happened, but every stinking church goer within a 300-mile radius ended up on post with me. They were great people, and their conversations drew me in.

Over time, I wondered what they knew about this church thing that I did not. It was not a pressing feeling, but all this time with these folks had softened me. I was not seeking or not googling churches, Jesus, or God, but this kind of non-churchy, real people had somehow lowered my guard. A few of my co-workers invited me to church with them, but I said no. I really did not want to go. And even if I did, I wanted to go on my own without any pressure to like it or put on a show for anyone.

So, one fateful Saturday evening, I snuck off to church (as my husband says), and it happened. It was amazing. I was filled with life and hope and wonder, and I encountered something I could not explain. But I wanted this presence with me for the rest of my life. I cannot tell you what the pastor spoke on that night, but one phrase rings in my heart even today. 'If you've never asked Jesus to come and live in your heart, but you want to, then raise your hand and repeat after me.'

The magnificent and amazing love and peace I felt that night was unlike anything else I had ever experienced. I was forever drawn in and longed to grow nearer and nearer to the One Who's Worthy, the Lamb of God Who loved me while I was yet a sinner, and Who desired to know me, though I am made from dirt. Can you imagine?

Ages before I arrived on this earth, eons before the cross, and eternities before the creation of the world—so long ago, before time began, in His absolute perfection and majesty, He imagined me. He dreamed about me. He pictured me in a specific place and time, fulfilling His magnificent purpose on the earth (and will continue this calling into Heaven). He anticipated me. He waited for me.

He waited for time, purpose, and history to intersect perfectly, and when that time came, He knit me together in my mother's womb and released me, all the while continuing to watching over, guiding, protecting, and prospering me.

What amazes me even still is He did not begin a relationship with me that autumn day. He only continued a relationship He had begun so many millennia before, but rather that one Texas evening, I was finally made aware of Him. Doesn't that just wreck you? It does me.

Many years before I ever knew Him, before I even acknowledged Him, He wooed me, like a lover woos his beloved. He was pleased to draw me to Himself one tiny moment at a time. Before I met God, and many years after, I did not realize I was playing a starring role in a story, which He would intertwine perfectly into His story. As I sit here now and think about my life in little life-moments, I see His fingerprints all over everyone and all over me.

It blew my mind then, and the more I know and encounter Him, the more undone I am. As I look back, I recall it was never on His terms, always on mine. To some, that may sound so wrong or even blasphemous, but it was so true for me. Here I am, nearly sixteen years later, and it's never changed. His kindness disarms me. His love captivates me. His peace settles me. His patience astounds me. His goodness persuades me. His joy draws me. He amazes me still. Each day, my greatest desire is to know Him as I am known.

Of course, I am not implying the unfathomable, incomprehensible, uncontainable Master and Creator of billions and billions of universes could ever be 'known,' but my heart's desire on this planet is to close that gap. One day,

I will know as completely as I am known, but today I will press to Him more because it is my joy and great pleasure to pursue Him. He is worth chasing. He is worth knowing. He is worth apprehending. And He is ecstatic to meet you.

I would love to introduce you to the Jesus I know if you will indulge me just a bit longer. There was a time when life kept me busy, and I had not spent nearly as much time with Him as I wanted or even needed. I felt bad for putting off my love and Lord during that time, and let Him know as I journaled this conversation:

> ***Me:*** *'Lord, I have not spent the time I need to with you lately. I am so sorry.'*
> ***Jesus:*** *'I miss you. I miss thinking with you and thinking through you. I miss being the object of your affection. I miss drawing near to you. I miss you.'*
> ***Me:*** *'I know, Lord. I am sorr...'*
> ***Jesus (interrupting):*** *'No. I miss you.'*
> ***Me:*** *'What? Okay. I am confused. I am sorry. You are right. I have not been...'*
> ***Jesus (interrupting, again):*** *'No! I have missed you. Don't you see? I am not trying to get a thing from you or out of you. I am not sad. I am not mad. I am sharing my feelings with you. It's what friends do. I miss you. I want you to know My heart. I love hanging out with you. I **love** it! You make My day. Shoot fire; you make My week! I miss those times. No condemnation. No underlying anything. I. Miss. You. Period. I am not like the world. That is not Me. I say what I mean, and My words carry weight. They possess depth and breadth*

*that you will only begin to understand this side of eternity. Dear and precious friend, they will **not** be laced with anything less than love, and mercy, and life, and gentleness. That is who I am. I cannot be anything less. I cannot become anything different. Beloved, I miss you.*

And do you know this is the exact same conversation Jesus would have with you? Whether, up until now, you have spent hours each day with him or hours each decade with Him, His conversation is the same; 'Dear and precious friend, I miss you.'"

~Dawn

You are loved just as you are. You are Father's favorite! Whether you have dedicated your whole life to following Him, or you are hearing this for the first time, you are still His favorite. May this just be a part of a beautiful journey of developing a relationship with your King and Creator.

Now I challenge you to write your own letter. What is God saying to you today? He has so many good things He wants to share with you because you are amazing. God's not afraid of our story, for He transforms it all for His glory. It has always been about humanity; it has always been about you. It has always been about love. Perfect, unhindered, restorative, beautiful love, and all we must do is receive.

Love letters desire action, so how do you respond?

"Dare to step past the limited vantage point of logic and into the wide expanse of faith-based belief."

BIBLIOGRAPHY

A, GCT. 2020. "Greek City Times." *The 8 Ancient Greek Words for Love* . February 14. Accessed December 2020. https://greekcitytimes.com/2020/02/14/the-8-ancient-greek-words-for-love/.

Antonucci, Vince. 2018. "City on a Hill." *He Is Jehovah Rapha and He's The God Who Heals*. December 11. Accessed December 2020. https://cityonahillstudio.com/he-is-jehovah-rapha-the-god-who-heals/.

Bartlett, Eugene. 1939. "Popular Hymns." *Victory In Jesus*. Accessed January 2021. https://popularhymns.com/victory-in-jesus.

BibleGateway. n.d. *Ephesians 2:19-21*. Accessed December 2020. https://www.biblegateway.com/passage/?search=Ephesians+2%3A19-21&version=NIV.

—. n.d. *John 14:15-17; 25-27*. Accessed January 2021. https://www.biblegateway.com/passage/?search=John+14%3A15-27+&version=NIV.

—. n.d. *John 3:7-20*. Accessed February 2021. https://www.biblegateway.com/passage/?search=John+3%3A7-20&version=NIV.

—. n.d. *John 4:1-26*. Accessed December 2020. https://www.biblegateway.com/passage/?search=John+4%3A1-26&version=NIV.

—. n.d. *John 5:1-16*. Accessed December 2020. https://www.biblegateway.com/passage/?search=John%205%3A1-16&version=NIV.

—. n.d. *Mark 5:15*. Accessed January 2021. https://www.biblegateway.com/passage/?search=Mark+5%3A15&version=NIV.

—. n.d. *Matthew 6:10*. Accessed January 2021. https://www.biblegateway.com/passage/?search=Matthew+6%3A10&version=NIV.

Bunnin, Nicholas, and Eric Tsui-James. 2008. *The Blackwell Companion to Philosophy pg 453*. John Wiley & Sons.

Card, Michael. 1983. *Tell the World that Jesus Loves You*. Comps. Michael Card and Randy Scruggs.

Carter, C Sue, and Stephen W Porges. 2012. "NCBI." *The biochemistry of love: an oxytocin hypothesis*. November 27. Accessed December 2020. https://www.ncbi.nlm.nih.gov/pmc/articles/PMC353 7144/.

Centers for Disease Control and Prevention. n.d. *Assault or Homicide*. Accessed November 2020. https://www.cdc.gov/nchs/fastats/homicide.htm.

Collins, Kathryn. 2018. "ResearchGate." *The Theory of Reality: A Critical & Philosophical Elaboration - DOI 10.35935/edr/24.2621*. April. Accessed 2021 January. https://www.researchgate.net/publication/33546780 9_The_Theory_of_Reality_A_Critical_Philosophical _Elaboration.

Deboer, Fredrik. 2016. "Foreign Policy." *America's Suicide Epidemic Is a National Security Crisis*. April 28. Accessed December 2020. https://foreignpolicy.com/2016/04/28/americas-suicide-epidemic-is-a-national-security-crisis/.

Denison, Dr. Jim. 2019. "Denison Forum." *Who Is the Holy Spirit?* August 24. Accessed January 2021. https://www.denisonforum.org/resource/faith-questions/who-is-the-holy-spirit/.

Descartes, Rene, Elizabeth Sanderson Haldane, and G R T Ross. 1911. *The Philosophical Works of Descartes*. Cambridge University Press.

Galtiere, Bill. n.d. "Soul Sheperding." *"Fear Not!" 365 Days a Year* . Accessed November 2020. https://www.soulshepherding.org/fear-not-365-days-a-year/.

May, Kate Torgovnick. 2012. "TedBlog." *5 insights from Brené Brown's new book, Daring Greatly, out today*. September 11. Accessed December 2020. https://blog.ted.com/5-insights-from-brene-browns-new-book-daring-greatly-out-today/.

McClure, Paul, and Hannah McClure. 2019. *Now I See - Bethel Music Publishing (ASCAP) Alletrop Music (BMI) (adm. at CapitolCMGPublishing.com)*. Comps. Paul McClure, Hannah McClure, Joel Taylor, Brian Johnson and Ed Cash. https://bethelmusic.com/chords-and-lyrics/now-i-see/.

Oxford Lexico. n.d. *Oxford Lexico*. Accessed December 2020. https://www.lexico.com/en/definition/identity.

—. n.d. *Peace*. Accessed January 2021. https://www.lexico.com/en/definition/peace.

—. n.d. *Reality*. Accessed January 2021. https://www.lexico.com/en/definition/reality.

Peters, J W. 2021. "Wikipedia." *Just Do It*. January 10. Accessed January 16, 2021. https://en.wikipedia.org/wiki/Just_Do_It#cite_note -nytimes-2.

Peters, Jeremy W. 2009. "The New York Times." *The Birth of 'Just Do It' and Other Magic Words*. August 19. Accessed January 2021. https://www.nytimes.com/2009/08/20/business/me dia/20adco.html.

Thaik, Dr. Cynthia. 2013. "Huffpost." *Love Heals!* July 6. Accessed December 2020. https://www.huffpost.com/entry/love-health- benefits_b_3131370.

Wikipedia. n.d. "Wikipidea." *Reality*. Accessed January 2021. https://en.wikipedia.org/wiki/Reality.

Wilkins, Todd Anson. 2009. "FaithLife Sermons." *Μέτρον (Metron)- Your Area Of Authority*. Accessed January 2021. https://sermons.faithlife.com/sermons/92736- metron-(metron)-your-area-of-authority.

Zantamata, Doe. 2019. *Happiness in Your Life - Book Three: Forgiveness*. Independently Published.

ABOUT THE AUTHOR

Allisun Wilbur began her journey on the Sunny East Coast of Florida, but she traded in her bathing suit for cowboy boots as a young adult. Crossing over to the Wild West, she has hung her hat in Amarillo, TX. By day she is a sugar hustler and certified Pastry Chef, and by night she is a Lego building, chicken taming, dance party instigating single mother. No matter which hat she may be wearing she is walking fully immersed in her purpose and identity of joy.

Writing allows her to tell the story of true, radical love that changed her life. Wanting to draw a clear line to the true author and finisher, this book contains a multitude of testimonies. The collaboration of voices speaks with triumphant authenticity of the hope found in the Grand Master of Design, God Almighty. Allisun's son, Kadin is very excited to follow in his mom's footsteps and now focuses on publishing his own book.

www.ingramcontent.com/pod-product-compliance
Lightning Source LLC
Chambersburg PA
CBHW061255120726
48001CB00001B/311